LEARNING THROUGH SIMULATIONS

Latest titles in the McGraw-Hill Training Series

SELF-DEVELOPMENT
A Facilitator's Guide
David Megginson and
Mike Pedler   ISBN 0-07-707460-2

DEVELOPING WOMEN THROUGH TRAINING
A Practical Handbook
Liz Willis and
Jenny Daisley   ISBN 0-07-707566-8

DESIGNING AND ACHIEVING COMPETENCY
A Competency-Based Approach to Developing People and
Organizations
Editors: Rosemary Boam
and Paul Sparrow   ISBN 0-07-707572-2

CLIENT-CENTRED CONSULTING
A Practical Guide for Internal Advisers and Trainers
Peter Cockman, Bill Evans
and Peter Reynolds   ISBN 0-07-707685-0

CAREER DEVELOPMENT AND PLANNING
A Guide for Managers, Trainers and Personnel Staff
Malcolm Peel   ISBN 0-07-707554-4

SALES TRAINING
A Guide to Developing Effective Salespeople
Frank S. Salisbury   ISBN 0-07-707458-0

TOTAL QUALITY TRAINING
The Quality Culture and Quality Trainer
Brian Thomas   ISBN 0-07-707472-6

TRAINING TO MEET THE TECHNOLOGY CHALLENGE
Trevor Bentley   ISBN 0-07-707589-7

IMAGINATIVE EVENTS Volumes I & II
Ken Jones   ISBN 0-07-707679-6 Volume I
                     ISBN 0-07-707680-X Volume II

Details of these and other titles in the series are available from:

The Product Manager, Professional Books, McGraw-Hill Book Company Europe, Shoppenhangers Road, Maidenhead, Berkshire, SL6 2QL, United Kingdom. Telephone: 0628 23432. Fax: 0628 770224

Learning through simulations

A guide to the design and use of simulations in business and education

John Fripp

McGRAW-HILL BOOK COMPANY

London · New York · St Louis · San Francisco · Auckland
Bogotá · Caracas · Hamburg · Lisbon · Madrid · Mexico · Milan
Montreal · New Delhi · Panama · Paris · San Juan · São Paulo
Singapore · Sydney · Tokyo · Toronto

Published by
McGRAW-HILL Book Company Europe
Shoppenhangers Road, Maidenhead, Berkshire, SL6 2QL, England
Telephone: 0628 23432
Fax: 0628 770224

British Library Cataloguing in Publication Data
Fripp, John William Ward
  Learning Through Simulations: Guide to
  the Design and Use of Simulations in
  Business and Education. — (McGraw-Hill
  Training Series)
  I. Title II. Series
  658.40352

ISBN 0-07-707588-9

Library of Congress Cataloging-in-Publication Data
Fripp, John
    Learning through simulations : a guide to the design and use of
  simulations in business and education / John Fripp.
      p.   cm.—(McGraw-Hill training series)
    Includes bibliographical references.
    ISBN 0-07-707588-9
    1. Executives—Training of—Simulation methods. 2. Management—
  Computer simulation. I. Title. II. Series.
  HD30.4.F74   1993
  650'.01'1—dc20   92-43603
                                                                      CIP

1234 CL 9543

Typeset by Book Ens Limited, Baldock, Herts
Printed and bound in Great Britain by Clays Ltd, St Ives plc

Contents

		Page
Series preface		vii
About the series editor		ix
Acknowledgements		x
Foreword		xi
1	**Why use business simulations?**	**1**
	Design and development	2
	The final product	6
	What are the benefits?	6
2	**What are simulations?**	**8**
	Operational simulations	10
	Behavioural simulations	16
	Financial simulations: risk analysis	17
	Simple simulations	18
	Characteristics of simulations	20
	References	22
3	**Business simulations in context**	**23**
	How business simulations differ	24
	Research into the practical uses of simulations	32
	Pros and cons of business simulations	33
	Conclusions	37
	References	37
4	**Approaches to learning**	**38**
	How do managers learn?	38
	What do managers need to learn?	42
	Learning methods	44
	How do the learning methods compare in practice?	53
	References	54
5	**The design process**	**55**
	Off-the-shelf or tailor-made?	56
	Designing a tailor-made simulation	58
	References and addresses	83

6   An example design—Stoke Mandeville Furniture   **84**
Stoke Mandeville Furniture   84
Designing the simulation   87

7   Running simulations   **97**
The administrator's roles   97
Types of use   99
Running the simulation   100
What can go wrong?   109
References   109

8   Case studies   **110**
Educational applications   110
Research applications   117
References   122

Further reading   **123**
Appendix 1   Documentation for the SMF simulation   **125**
Appendix 2   Simulation suppliers and typical products **162**
Index   **178**

Series preface

Training and development are now firmly centre stage in most organizations, if not all. Nothing unusual in that—for some organizations. They have always seen training and development as part of the heart of their businesses—but more and more must see it the same way.

The demographic trends through the nineties will inject into the marketplace severe competition for good people who will need good training. Young people without conventional qualifications, skilled workers in redundant crafts, people out of work, women wishing to return to work—all will require excellent training to fit them to meet the job demands of the 1990s and beyond.

But excellent training does not spring from what we have done well in the past. T&D specialists are in a new ball game. 'Maintenance' training—training to keep up skill levels to do what we have always done—will be less in demand. Rather, organization, work and market change training are now much more important and will remain so for some time. Changing organizations and people is no easy task, requiring special skills and expertise which, sadly, many T&D specialists do not possess.

To work as a 'change' specialist requires us to get to centre stage—to the heart of the company's business. This means we have to ask about future goals and strategies and even be involved in their development, at least as far as T&D policies are concerned.

This demands excellent communication skills, political expertise, negotiating ability, diagnostic skills—indeed, all the skills a good internal consultant requires.

The implications for T&D specialists are considerable. It is not enough merely to be skilled in the basics of training, we must also begin to act like business people and to think in business terms and talk the language of business. We must be able to resource training not just from within but by using the vast array of external resources. We must be able to manage our activities as well as any other manager. We must share in the creation and communication of the company's vision. We must never let the goals of the company out of our sight.

In short, we may have to grow and change with the business. It will be hard. We shall not only have to demonstrate relevance but also value for money and achievement of results. We shall be our own boss, as accountable for results as any other line manager, and we shall have to deal with fewer internal resources.

The challenge is on, as many T&D specialists have demonstrated to me over the past few years. We need to be capable of meeting that challenge. This is why McGraw-Hill Book Company Europe have planned and launched this major new training series—to help us meet that challenge.

The series covers all aspects of T&D and provides the knowledge base from which we can develop plans to meet the challenge. They are practical books for the professional person. They are a starting point for planning our journey into the twenty-first century.

Use them well. Don't just read them. Highlight key ideas, thoughts, action pointers or whatever, and have a go at doing something with them. Through experimentation we evolve; through stagnation we die.

I know that all the authors in the McGraw-Hill Training Series would want me to wish you good luck. Have a great journey into the twenty-first century.

ROGER BENNETT
Series Editor

About the series editor

Roger Bennett has over 20 years' experience in training, management education, research and consulting. He has long been involved with trainer training and trainer effectiveness. He has carried out research into trainer effectiveness and conducted workshops, seminars and conferences on the subject around the world. He has written extensively on the subject including the book *Improving Trainer Effectiveness*, Gower. His work has taken him all over the world and has involved directors of companies as well as managers and trainers.

Roger Bennett has worked in engineering, several business schools (including the International Management Centre, where he launched the UK's first masters degree in T&D) and has been a board director of two companies. He is the editor of the *Journal of European Industrial Training* and was series editor of the ITD's *Get In There* workbook and video package for the managers of training departments. He now runs his own business called The Management Development Consultancy.

Acknowledgements

I would like to express my sincere thanks to the many people who have helped me to write this book. Firstly to my colleagues at Ashridge Management College, from whom I have learned a great deal about how managers learn, about the place of simulations in this process and about much else. Many of them have also willingly acted as guinea pigs on the many occasions when I have tried out new simulations. Thanks are also due to the numerous course members who have participated in my simulations over the years.

A number of colleagues have been especially helpful in the preparation of the material contained in this book. Jackie Ashton helped me to develop my ideas for the example simulation described in Chapter 6, and Kevin Barham made some much appreciated comments on managerial learning and on competences. Tracy Bowdrey-Long typed the final drafts of the text. I would particularly like to single out Martin Bennett who added his financial expertise to the description of the simulation described in Chapter 6 and in Appendix 1 and improved it enormously.

I would also like to thank many individuals in the companies for whom I have consulted over the years, who have allowed me to put my ideas into practice by cooperating in the design and development of tailor-made simulations. In particular my thanks are due to Neil Smith of British Aerospace, Ms J Waters of the Home Office and Michael Blackstad, Chief Executive of Workhouse Productions, for permission to describe case studies in Chapter 8.

May I also thank the series editor, Roger Bennett, who first encouraged me to write the book, and my publishers, Jenny Ertle, James Hyde and Julia Riddlesdell for their constant support and patience until it was completed, and in particular for their help in conducting the survey of simulation users.

Finally I must express a heartfelt thank you to my wife and family for their forbearance over many months. While I have been writing this book they have done many of the other things that I should have been doing. Thank you all.

JOHN FRIPP
Leighton Buzzard

Foreword

Simulations and games have been used in education for a long time. Apart from being fun, they give a very useful insight into a variety of business and social processes. Properly used, simulations can be powerful and flexible educational devices, and computer-based business simulations have a particular part to play in this. The widespread availability of personal computers means that every organization can now make use of them. However, there are a huge number and variety of simulations and games available on the market, and this means that information on them is not always easily available. This book will help to fill that need.

Although generally well regarded, simulations are not as widely used nor as well used as they might be. This book is intended to give users and potential users of business simulations an insight into some of the many ways that simulations can be used, and how to ensure that they are chosen carefully for the circumstances in which they will be used.

Chapter 1 begins by telling the story of a particular organization which developed a tailor-made simulation for training senior executives. This case study acts as an introduction to the book as a whole and describes the reasons why the simulation was developed, the steps that were taken to design it, and the benefits that were gained.

Chapter 2 compares and contrasts a range of different simulations and draws out their common features. Chapter 3 discusses the merits of computer-based and manually-based simulations. It also contains the results of a specially-commissioned survey to discover the views of training and management development managers on simulations.

Chapter 4 deals with the central subject of how managers learn, and the part that simulations and other learning methods such as lectures and case studies play in this process. The strengths and weaknesses of various learning methods are compared. Chapter 5 explains the process that has to be undertaken to design a simulation, especially one tailored for a particular training need and for a particular organization.

Chapter 6 contains an example of this design process, and shows how a business simulation can be designed to represent a set of issues facing a fictitious small manufacturing company. The company and some of the key issues it faces are first described qualitatively, and then by using some simple methods, they are described in ways that are suitable for a program to be developed. Chapter 7 gives practical advice on how to run simulations more effectively.

The final chapter broadens out the discussion again by describing a number of case studies in which business simulations have been used for various purposes, including the development of teamworking skills, the exploration of corporate strategy, and for other educational and business research purposes. Finally, several recommendations are made for the future direction of simulations.

Appendix 1 contains a set of documentation for the simulation developed in Chapter 6. These will act both as examples of the kind of documentation needed for simulations, and also give fuller detail for those wishing to develop their own copy of the simulation described in Chapter 6. The second appendix contains an annotated list of simulation suppliers in the UK, the USA and elsewhere, and includes descriptions of some of their most popular products.

Those concerned with the wider application of experience-based learning will find much of interest to them, since simulations are not just concerned with imitating the known; they are capable of placing people in novel circumstances, and of stretching their experiences and capabilities in new and unexpected ways. At a time when training managers and others are concerned with ever more relevant approaches to management development and training, this book will come as a timely reminder of the advantages which simulations offer for learning, giving guidance on how to maximize their potential.

1 Why use business simulations?

The 1980s were difficult and turbulent years and like many other firms at the time, a leading insurance company experienced radical changes in business conditions. The company had until recently been very successful in developing its business using aggressive marketing policies. Then the emphasis changed as profit margins began to shrink and stringent financial controls became necessary. Company executives adjusted to the needs of the new conditions. A few years later conditions changed again, and the same executives were faced with clients who were becoming much more demanding and who insisted on superior standards of service. This meant the company had to have a genuine commitment to high quality in all areas of the business and a new focus on delivering those standards of service through greater professionalism and improved communications skills.

Throughout this time the company had maintained its belief in the value of management development activities and had been closely associated with Ashridge Management College. Working with the company, Ashridge had designed a range of tailor-made courses for directors and senior managers, among which was one on financial awareness. This course had two main aims. One was to sharpen business and financial skills in order to give managers greater control over their own businesses and the second was to help them understand the wide variety of financial circumstances faced by their clients, thus leading to a deeper insight into clients' particular insurance needs.

This chapter tells the true story of how and why the company used a computer-based business simulation as part of this course. A simulation was used rather than other approaches to management training as it was believed to be a more effective learning medium for executives who were much more used to being active and 'doing' than to passively listening. The business simulation formed an important part of the course and its purpose was to give participants a better understanding of what makes for success in a complex, changing commercial environment. The company had its own jargon and reporting systems, and the simulation used these to produce the type of management reports and accounts which were employed in the company. These were quite different from most company reporting systems and from the general purpose simulation which had previously been used on the course.

The course used a variety of different learning methods, including lectures and case studies and the general purpose simulation mentioned above. These had achieved considerable success, but the company was keen to develop a simulation that mirrored their own type of business more closely. So the existing simulation was replaced by the tailor-made one. Users' comments have shown that the exercise was thoroughly worth while. Subsequent developments have ensured that the simulation is kept up to date.

Design and development

The simulation was sponsored by the chief executive of the insurance company, whose aim was to ensure the executives became even more aware of the various forces that governed the successful running of an insurance business, particularly during changing circumstances. Some of these circumstances, for example general economic conditions and interest rates, were naturally outside their control, but a rapid and appropriate response to them was essential to business success. It was also necessary for participants to really understand the type of business they were engaged in, and the company's prevailing business strategy. They had to get fully involved in the debate about whether the current strategy was appropriate in the changing business conditions, and if not, what needed to be done to make the business move in the desired direction.

The simulation was developed after an extensive period of consultation with several company senior managers. The main design work was carried out by a small team consisting of the author, the company finance director and another insurance executive. Both company executives, apart from being knowledgeable about their own company and the industry generally, were able to think in conceptual terms about the kind of business issues that should be included in the simulation and how these could be represented.

The simulation was designed to represent a number of competing insurance companies, each to be run by a group of course members. Typically there would be three or four teams taking part in the exercise, each comprising four to six executives. The simulation represented several different types of insurance business, which were naturally simplified compared with reality. These included:

• private insurance (e.g. domestic and other insurance offered to private individuals)
• commercial insurance (e.g. fire insurance on commercial premises)

The design team then debated the major factors which influenced the number of clients the company could attract within the above types of business, and the resultant costs and profitability. The discussions centred on the best way to attract and keep clients of each type. As in reality, there was a fairly well-defined set of issues which were within the control of simulation participants, and others which would remain outside their control. Among the latter were the level of premiums appropriate to each type of insurance business, and the proportion of these which the company could charge as fees for their own services. Both these were set by industry norms.

After the first couple of meetings of the design team the author produced a draft specification highlighting the following crucial points:

- the influence participants would have in the simulation (i.e. the decisions they would be required to make)
- the amount of freedom and constraints that participants should have in making these decisions
- preliminary ideas on how the various decisions would affect the client base and profitability of each team
- the amount and type of information, of both an operational and a financial nature, that the simulation would produce
- the appearance of the financial and other results

The team met periodically over the next few months and the simulation was gradually refined. The author began programming when the draft specification was agreed, but the programme naturally underwent many changes. Figure 1.1 shows in simplified form some of the major issues that were eventually agreed to influence the company's share of the commercial insurance market, and how these issues were interrelated.

Particular attention was paid to the presentation of the financial statements. Some managers were new to the company and therefore did not have long experience of parent company accounting systems. The simulation deliberately presented accounts in the 'approved' way, using the kind of performance ratios and terminology employed in the parent

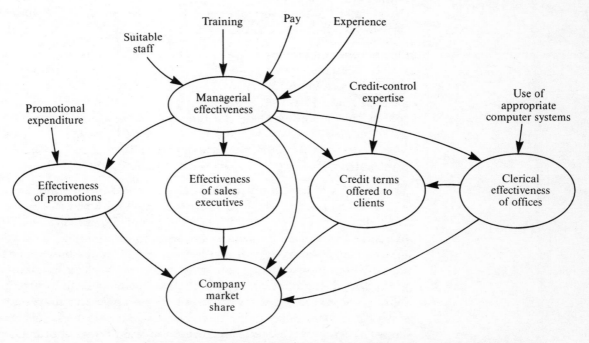

Figure 1.1 Issues and relationships in a simplified commercial insurance market

company's own management accounts. This was to prove a valuable learning opportunity for all participants.

Discussions also centred around the economic environment, and the extent to which the simulation should mirror current or predicted future conditions. Eventually it was agreed that the first few years of the simulation should be close to previous operating conditions, and that these should be presented to participants as background material. The simulation would then start on familiar ground, but conditions during the years in which participants played the simulation would then be allowed to diverge from strict reality, within reasonable limits. This would equip participants with experience of more or less favourable trading conditions, and give them some feel for the likely consequences of their actions on company performance.

Personnel issues were not forgotten. The simulation was designed to include several types of staff, and a range of important personnel matters. Realistic staffing and pay levels were included, as were matters relating to training and recruitment, and the inevitable loss of staff through natural turnover. The latter led to another vital personnel issue which was how the company could attract and motivate the right calibre of high quality staff, particularly in the important sales executive role. Sales executives were the people who made most direct contact with clients and potential clients, and whose professionalism was vital to success. They were critical in determining the kind of impression that clients had of the company, and on the standards of service the company offered its clients. Within the confines of the game it was not possible to reflect all of the many personal qualities and skills necessary to perform this job successfully, but a number of important organizational and personnel issues which did affect the quality of sales executives were included.

One necessary simplification was that participants in the simulation would set salaries for all grades of staff in their simulated companies with reference to one salary only, rather than having a separate salary for each grade. However, it was felt necessary to distinguish between professional and other grades for the purpose of natural wastage, since levels differed in reality. In the simulation natural wastage was made to respond to the types of factors that were important in reality, including comparative salaries, or the availability of training.

The directors of each company were also included in the simulation, and were represented by the participants themselves. One issue for the directors was how they should spend their limited time. They essentially had three kinds of duties. One was to work as senior sales executives, making new business contacts and helping to develop the business in this way. The second was to help service existing clients, ensuring that their needs were being fully met and thereby maintaining client loyalty. The third was to devote themselves to a largely administrative function by supervising the running of the business and their own staff. This latter course of action was more likely to result in good financial control but many found it less rewarding than client contact.

The company had been successful in growing by making a number of acquisitions. It had brought together a number of hitherto independent companies, each coming from a different background and each with its own history and culture, but all now a part of the same group. Acquisitions continued to be an important issue and they were therefore included as part of the simulation. It was decided that at periodic intervals during the simulation each company would be given the opportunity to acquire another business. As in real life, however, not every candidate for acquisition would be suitable, and not every company acquired would turn out to be profitable. Many hours of debate ensued in which the design team discussed the issues that would determine how a potential candidate could be judged, and what were the really critical issues determining post-acquisition success. Of course, some of the real-life issues could not easily be included within the scope of the simulation, but many were included, sometimes in a simplified form.

It was here that a colleague of the author played a vital role. He knew the major players in the insurance industry well, and was familiar with their financial strengths and weaknesses. He produced a set of fictitious company reports, each loosely based on a real-life company and each giving the reason why the company was available for acquisition. The reports gave a brief and often humorous background to the company concerned and contained the last couple of years' accounts. They also gave the current client portfolio and each company's perceived strengths and weaknesses. Participants often recognized the actual company on which each report was built, but had to analyse the information carefully to see if the company was right for them, and if so, how much to bid to acquire it.

Acquisitions were only one way to expand the business. Another was by continued marketing activities, perhaps accompanied by the purchase of additional premises and the hiring and training of the necessary high quality staff, and by the continued focus on the provision of high quality services. These alternative approaches to growth and profitability were also represented within the simulation.

The first trial run of the simulation was attended by members of the design team, by colleagues of the author and by managers from the company's personnel and training department. Both the design team and company managers felt that the major issues were adequately modelled, bearing in mind the level of participants for whom the simulation was designed, and the context in which the simulation was to be used. As a result of the trial several adjustments were made to the simulation and the first real test occurred a while later during one of the company's finance courses. Both company executives who had assisted in the design and the chief executive were present on this and on subsequent occasions, to add credibility to the exercise and to explain some of the finer points to course members.

The final product

The final product is a simulation program and a comprehensive set of documentation for both participants and administrators. Each team starts with the same portfolio of clients and with the same assets and liabilities. This situation does not continue long, however, as teams soon develop different aims and objectives, and set about developing their businesses in their own way.

A major problem facing participants is to agree exactly how to mobilize their efforts to attract more business in selected business sectors. How can this be achieved within limited financial resources? Each simulated year, participants have to make a series of routine decisions, including:

- how the directors will spend their time
- how many sales executives and other staff are required, and how these will be remunerated
- the quality of service that will be offered to new or existing clients, measured in various ways
- the expenditure on advertising and promotions
- developments in the branch network

In addition, every few years, one of the fictitious companies is presented for acquisition. Each team is given the same set of information about the company and a lively discussion ensues. Will the company fit in with our own declared aims? How sound is it? If we acquire the company what will it do for us? How much should we be prepared to pay for it? Sealed bids are then collected and the highest bid is accepted, subject to the reserve price being exceeded. All the decisions, including the successful bids for acquisitions, are then processed by the simulation program and results are presented to each team. Participants are invariably anxious to see the results they have achieved and often queue up to receive them. The simulation results in an active and keenly contested couple of days.

What are the benefits?

The simulation program was initially written for a minicomputer, but was subsequently transferred to an IBM-compatible personal computer for ease of use and portability. It has been run in a variety of locations with great success and has been used by over 100 senior executives. It is preceded in the course by other material of a mainly financial nature. The simulation is the final major activity in the course, and is used as an illustration of many of the ideas that have already been discussed.

The exercise provides the opportunity that not many other management development activities do; the chance to try out new ideas and approaches to real business problems in a safe, simulated environment, and receive feedback in unmistakable financial terms. Case studies are very useful for studying particular incidents, illustrating 'best practice', or indeed showing how to avoid mistakes, but they are not dynamic in the sense that they do not give participants the opportunity to live through the consequences of their own actions.

Managers involved in the simulation usually disagree on what is the appropriate course of action, and sometimes heated discussion continues long after the allotted time is up. This is normally a good sign, indicating that the exercise has succeeded in bringing to the surface the very issues for which it and the course were designed.

Business simulations are not new, but they have not always been as well used as they might be, perhaps because they do not always represent closely enough the realities of the organization concerned. The above example shows that with suitable cooperation, an appropriate degree of reality can be achieved. The company is certainly happy with the exercise. The chief executive has stated categorically that he knows no other way to allow executives to experience the commercial problems of a decade in a few hours, and that the learning curve provided by the simulation is 'steep indeed'. As far as participants themselves are concerned, the whole exercise seems to have been worth while. Comments have shown that the simulation:

- 'is a very useful experience in assessing the value of acquisitions'
- 'is very enjoyable and informative'
- 'brings together the course well'
- 'provides for good group discussion'
- 'enables us to use the knowledge gained earlier'

Since the simulation was designed the business conditions in which the insurance company operates have changed yet again. The focus of the simulation has therefore shifted both in terms of the types of client the company deals with and the issues that have to be faced to satisfy their needs profitably. Several new major decision areas have been incorporated, and some previous ones left out. There have of course been continuing changes in interest rates, pay rates and inflation. For all these reasons the simulation has undergone continuous development in order to mirror the new conditions.

2 What are simulations?

Whenever we are faced with a complex problem in business, in design or in engineering, there are usually several ways to find a solution. If the problem is a familiar one, we can use well-tried practical methods that have succeeded before. If it is novel, and no ready-made solution exists, other approaches are necessary. We may understand the problem sufficiently well to develop a solution from existing knowledge, or perhaps we can simply guess an answer and try it out. If neither approach is possible because of the complexity of the problem, or because of the risks involved, then the technique of simulation may be the only way forward.

Simulations are used for many reasons, but their main purpose is to help to understand and solve complex real-life problems by constructing a small, simplified version of the problem, often called a 'model'. The model can be more easily understood than the real thing. We can manipulate the model to see how it behaves much more safely than we could intervene in the real problem, and this can often take us a long way towards solving the problem.

A good example of simulation is a wind tunnel used to test a newly-designed aircraft. The new aircraft is usually different in a number of important ways from current designs, so it may well behave quite differently in flight. Predicting its flying characteristics is too complex a problem to trust to existing aeronautical theory, and it is obviously too risky to build the aircraft without first testing a model in realistic conditions. Hence the need for wind tunnel testing, where we simulate real flying conditions in the safety of a laboratory.

Another example is a flight simulator, in which a pilot is put through the 'experience' of flying an aircraft without the risk or the expense of flying the real thing. In business too, simulations are used in a variety of ways. For example, the technique may be used to investigate the likely profitability of a major project before making the decision to proceed. It may also be used to help understand how best to lay out a new production plant before starting construction, to ensure that production can be carried out smoothly and efficiently. In the last two cases it is not necessary to construct a physical model, since we can usually study the problems better by using a different kind of model, one consisting essentially of a series of mathematical equations in a computer program.

popular in 90's

Computer-based business simulations are also increasingly being used for education and training purposes, and a wide variety of simulations or games are now available. This increase has partly been brought about by the widespread availability of personal computers, and partly due to the search for practical educational methods. We now describe several different examples of simulations to show how widely the technique has been used and to underline the common features of all simulations. The first example is the aircraft flight simulator mentioned above.

Aircraft flight simulators

The increasing sophistication of modern aircraft means that it is essential to train pilots to very high standards. Aircraft navigation and control systems demand ever higher levels of expertise. Pilots can of course learn a great deal about flying, aerodynamics, flight control systems and safety procedures without going anywhere near a real aircraft, or indeed a simulator. They can learn the theory in a variety of ways: by attending classes, by observation, talking to experts, and studying appropriate literature. However, what really matters is the ability to put the knowledge into practice. Unfortunately real aircraft are often too scarce to let all trainee pilots have access to them throughout their training, and it can be too risky to do so. Hence the need for flight simulators.

The simulator represents the operation of a particular type of aircraft with a high degree of realism. The trainees can be subjected to a wide range of normal and abnormal flying conditions, and their performances are closely monitored. They can make mistakes in the course of this training without anyone suffering the consequences, and when mistakes are made the simulation can be repeated with exactly the same set of conditions to ensure that lessons have been learned and that performance improves.

Flight simulators are, of course, not used just for trainee pilots. They are invaluable for testing and updating the skills of experienced pilots, and for giving additional training necessary to enable a pilot qualified on one type of aircraft to fly another one. They can be used for other purposes apart from training. They are also used in research programs, for example to study the reaction of pilots to particular types of cockpit display, or to learn more about their performance under conditions of stress or fatigue. In this case the simulator would need to be designed rather differently to ensure that it was possible to reproduce the particular circumstances of interest, such as a change in the layout or design of the control panel or instrumentation, or to introduce the kind of stressful conditions required. The pilot's performance would have to be monitored even more closely than in a training simulator in order to assess his or her reactions accurately. Thus simulations can have more than one purpose, and we will return to this theme in later chapters.

Realism

Seen from the outside, the aircraft flight simulator looks like a large irregularly-shaped metallic box supported on hydraulic stilts, with various cables hanging from it. Unlike a real aircraft, it has no wings, it is bolted firmly to the floor and in many ways it is wholly unrealistic. Once inside, however, we quickly gain a different impression. From the inside it looks very much like a real aircraft flight deck, complete with all the dials and indicators, and with a forward display shown on a set of video screens. These are programmed to give exactly the same view the pilot would have in a real aircraft, including for example the position of the aircraft relative to the runway on landing or takeoff.

When in action the pilot has no doubt that the simulator behaves very much like the real aircraft. It responds realistically to all the pilot's actions and enables the pilot to face most of the problems that would occur in a real flight. The trainer running the simulation has total control over the aircraft and its environment, and can vary the weather conditions at will or mimic a failure in some part of the aircraft equipment. Thus a variety of conditions can be introduced, some of which might be met only rarely in the natural course of events, but which the pilot must master as part of training.

While not having all the features of the aircraft it is intended to portray, the flight simulator does have the essential advantage of behaving in the required way. It can represent a far wider range of flying conditions than would be encountered in many years flying. It gives pilots the opportunity to practise difficult operations which happen only rarely, often interspersed with long periods of monotony. So elaborate are flight simulators that their operating costs are similar to those of a real aircraft. So although the simulator can never be totally realistic, it is realistic enough for its purpose. Even those readers who have used a simple flight simulator on a home computer will have experienced a little of that realism.

Operational simulations

An operational simulation is designed to show the performance of people, plant or equipment under a variety of different operating conditions. An operational simulation sometimes involves the construction of a physical model of the problem under study, such as the flight simulator or a wind tunnel. More often, however, this is not necessary and all the important features are represented in a computer model. The latter approach is used in a manufacturing organization when the simulation may be designed to show the effects of different production control methods on the output of a factory.

Another example is the design of a dock where the designers need to make best use of available resources including staff, money, equipment or space, and are therefore anxious to arrange the physical layout of berths and loading and unloading facilities in the best way possible. In a dock simulation the computer model is used to show the effects of changing key variables, such as layout of the docks, the capacity of cranes, and different ship arrival rates, in order to establish the best possible operating arrangements. In this and many such cases an operational simulation is the only way of representing the complexities of the real-life situation, as we simply would not contemplate the construction of a multi-million pound dock without testing the design first.

A further example arises in planning a new telephone exchange. Here one of the major problems is how to deal with varying customer demands. It would not be realistic to assume that there will be a known and fixed number of telephone calls per hour, and that each customer will require exactly the same length of time for his or her call to be completed satisfactorily. In reality both call frequency and call duration vary from one caller to another and from one day to another in an unpredictable way. We would therefore make gross errors in designing the exchange if we ignored these variations, leading to an exchange which did not give customers the level of service that was intended. On the other hand, to assume the worst and that the maximum number of calls will occur each day, and that these will all last the maximum length of time, may well give callers a superb standard of service, but at enormous cost to the supplier. In this case the numbers of telephone lines and telephonists would be based upon conditions which would only occur rarely in practice, and resources would therefore be largely unused except in peak conditions.

Under suitable circumstances there are ready-made tables which can be used to provide guidance on the required number of telephonists or lines to give any required level of service. However, these are only applicable where the call durations and frequencies obey certain mathematical laws. Where this is not the case then the approach is invalid, and simulation methods must be used.

Where the representation of random events is an important feature of a simulation, such as in the telephone exchange, the term 'Monte Carlo' simulation is sometimes used, due to the analogy of the roulette wheel as a means of producing random numbers. Sequences of random numbers are used in Monte Carlo simulations to represent all the important random influences that occur in the real problem. We now briefly describe an example of the Monte Carlo simulation of a telephone exchange.

A simulation of a telephone exchange

What information do we need to simulate the operation of a telephone exchange? There are essentially two types: information on the demands placed upon the service by customers or potential customers, and information on the operating procedures proposed by those running the exchange. In the first case, we need to know, or estimate, the number of customers who will call us, hour by hour throughout the working day, and how these are distributed, i.e. whether people are likely to call at regular intervals, or whether the frequency of calls will vary through time. Similarly we need to know the distribution of the length of time customers will require on the telephone. The second type of information implies knowledge of how the exchange will be operated, for example how many telephone lines and telephonists there will be, whether a call queueing system will be used, and the nature of customer calls. Table 2.1 shows a simple example of the distribution of the number of

customers who call us per hour. For simplicity we will assume the distribution applies to every hour of the working day.

Table 2.1 *Distribution of the number of calls per hour*

Calls per hour	Probability (%)
1 to 10	10
11 to 20	20
21 to 30	30
31 to 40	20
41 to 50	10
51 to 100	10

Table 2.1 shows that the exchange is most likely to receive between 21
and 30 calls per hour, but any number between one and a hundred are
possible. There is for example a 10 per cent chance that we will receive
between 51 and 100 calls in an hour. Table 2.2 shows the distribution of
the length of time each customer will spend on the telephone. The most
likely call length is from 2.1 to 5.0 minutes, but calls lasting up to 30
minutes are possible.

Table 2.2 *Distribution of call durations*

Call duration (minutes)	Probability (%)
0 – 2.0	20
2.1 – 5.0	40
5.1 – 8.0	20
8.1 – 15.0	10
15.1 – 30.0	10

In order to gather this type of data we would have to spend considerable
time with those responsible for the exchange, or a similar one, to ensure
that the two distributions are a good representation of what is expected
in reality. We would then discuss the proposed working of the
exchange to ensure we understand how calls are to be dealt with. The
next step is to construct a flowchart showing how the whole telephone
exchange works, as shown in a simplified way in Figure 2.1. Time is
represented by a clock which moves forward one minute at a time over
any required time period.

A program is then developed to simulate the exchange using data from
the distributions shown in Tables 2.1 and 2.2. The computer program
would follow the flowchart and carry out the necessary calculations. The
simulation may need to be run for a considerable number of simulated
days, since we have to allow a large number of random events to occur
in order to represent the full range of data. During any one simulation

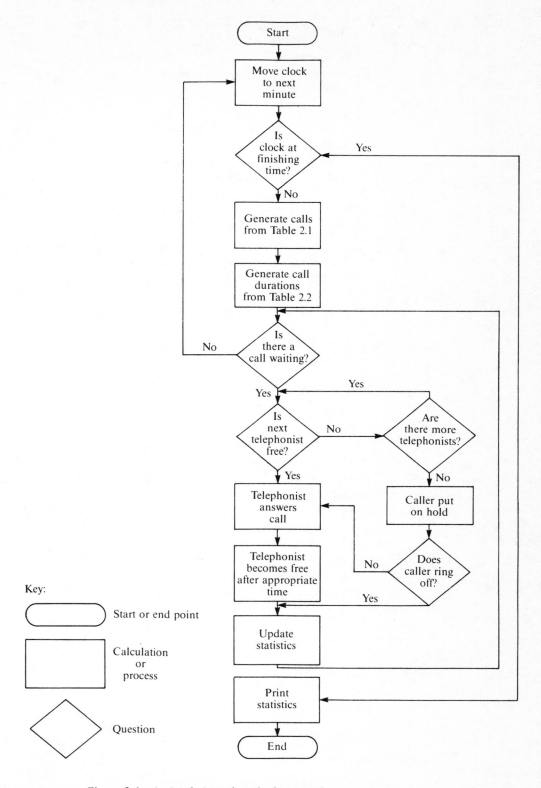

Figure 2.1 A simulation of a telephone exchange

we may have chosen, purely by chance, a set of values which are untypical. During the simulation we record the results that are of interest, for example, the number of telephonists working, and the time it takes for each caller to have his or her call answered. We also record the number of customers who ring off in disgust because their call was not answered promptly.

Note that we must still use the concept of a 'distribution' of values to record the results of the simulation. We might use simple averages for communication with customers, but we would require more detail than that to make sensible decisions on the allocation of resources. For example, we often need the worst case to ensure we understand the implications of a policy such as 'we answer all calls within 30 seconds'.

The simulation is then repeated by varying the number of operators or lines until we obtain a satisfactory combination of cost and service. Figure 2.2 shows a typical set of results from such a simulation showing that the addition of more and more telephonists and lines adds to the cost of the system, as shown by the straight line and right-hand scale. However, the simulation will show the level of service given to customers, in this case the proportion of calls answered in a given time. According to the procedures in use and the number of telephonists, this will vary in a more complex way, as shown by the curve and left-hand scale.

Results of the simulation show how well the whole exchange system is performing, from both the customers' and the operators' points of view. Note, however, that personal judgement is still required to decide on the number of telephonists in order to arrive at an appropriate tradeoff between the cost of supplying more telephonists and the resultant increased level of service offered, and the 'cost' of dissatisfied customers. Even if it were possible to establish an overall minimum cost solution, judgement would still be necessary to make the final choice. But the simulation will have thrown considerable light on how the exchange functions. Note, however, that in all operational simulations

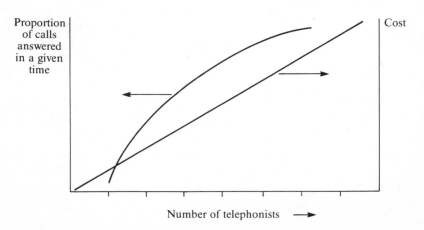

Figure 2.2   Typical simulation results

the results are only as good as the quality of the data used, and the accuracy of the operating procedures we simulate.

An insurance simulation

Another example is taken from the world of insurance, where risk clearly plays a central role. Computer-based simulation techniques have been used to investigate the performance of insurance companies under a wide range of different circumstances. In essence the purpose is identical to an aircraft designer testing the design of a new aircraft in a wind tunnel, except that here the users may be concerned about the viability of certain new insurance schemes, or other business ventures.

This type of operational simulation needs a great deal of information about the economy, the special features of the insurance market, and the company concerned. Particular uncertain issues might be future interest and inflation rates, competitors' actions, and market growth rates. The model allows management to try out a number of different approaches, for example to vary the insurance rates on offer and the type of risk covered. Random events such as the number of claims in any year must be included. The users of the simulation are therefore able to investigate the financial performance of an insurance company under a wide range of conditions. Management can also answer a number of important questions of a strategic nature, including the effect of increasing premiums by more or less than inflation, the effects of placing funds in long-term or short-term investments, or delaying premium rises for a year.

Company managers can use such a simulation to explore a wider range of future scenarios than might otherwise be possible. With suitable amendments the simulation can also be used for training purposes. Here the participants would make a number of decisions and the simulation would show the results of these. Each time the process is repeated participants would thus gain further experience and insight, as was shown in Chapter 1.

A manpower planning simulation

Many organizations have used simulations for manpower planning. The purpose is often to help predict the impact of recruitment and other manpower decisions upon future staff levels. These simulations require information on the current number of staff available in each grade, the details of the grade structure and possible movements between grades, and the future numbers of staff required at each level.

 Assumptions must also be made about future natural wastage rates. These will be partly speculative, and may depend on seniority or age of the employees or their length of service. It will also depend on external factors such as unemployment levels and pay rates in other organizations. Since the data used in these simulations are estimates for some years in the future, they can be expressed either as single values or as distributions.

Users normally run the model a number of times, each time making a set of decisions, for example on future recruitment and promotions. The model then calculates the effects of these decisions, usually over a two- to five-year period. Results show whether or not the required manpower levels can be met from existing staff, and how much further recruitment or promotion will be necessary.

The limitation of this type of approach is that the model reflects purely quantitative issues, namely the comparison of future supply and demand for certain categories of staff. The issue of the quality of staff is not addressed directly. However, even within these limitations the simulation can give illuminating and sometimes unexpected results, for example to indicate promotion bottlenecks in certain grades, manpower shortages in others, or some unexpected interactions between different manpower policies.

Behavioural simulations

A good example of a totally different, non computer-based simulation is the 'Desert Survival' exercise (Lafferty and Pond, 1986). This is designed to illustrate group behaviour, face-to-face communications, listening and teamworking skills.

Participants are placed in groups of six to eight and are asked to imagine that they are passengers in an aircraft that has crash-landed in a desert. They are unhurt, but they are unable to contact the outside world, and due to an instrument fault, the aircraft has been flying off-course for some time and no one else knows where they are. Participants therefore have no immediate hope of rescue, although a rescue attempt will obviously be mounted once they are reported missing.

The group is then told that they have a number of articles which have also survived the crash, including an aerial map of the desert, a parachute, a revolver, a bottle of vodka and a mirror. They are instructed that they must stay together as a group, and they are faced with a number of decisions. Firstly, will they stay with the aircraft, or will they move off and attempt to find their way back to civilization? They also have to rank the various articles in order of importance. Groups are given a fixed time in which to perform this task.

The exercise can be run in a number of ways. One method is to allow each individual to rank the articles in his or her preferred order before any discussion. Discussion then ensues to decide whether or not to leave the aircraft, and to agree on a group ranking of the articles. The various objects have been ranked in order of usefulness by a desert survival expert. Thus individuals and groups have an external objective measure against which they can compare their own results. A simple scoring method shows the extent of agreement or disagreement with the expert solution. The exercise is non-interactive between groups, except that each group obviously wants to get as close to the expert's view as possible. It is normal to compare the average individual score before discussion with the group consensus score after discussion. Usually the group score is better than the average individual score, showing the positive advantages of working in groups.

Although deceptively simple, the exercise is behaviourally a very rich one. A skilled observer is needed to make the best use of the exercise and sensitively feed back observations to the group, ideally with the aid of a video recording of the proceedings. Several different issues can be highlighted according to the purpose of the exercise. A variety of similar exercises are now available including Alaskan Adventure, Sub-Arctic Survival, Jungle Escape, Carribean Island Survival and Whitewater.

Another example of a widely used behavioural simulation is 'Looking Glass' (Lombardo *et al*, 1976), an exercise based on an imaginary company in the glass manufacturing industry. The simulation usually takes place over a complete day, and participants play the parts of top managers. They are given an annual report and realistic background data on the operations of the company. The detailed information contained in each participant's brief differs somewhat from position to position and from division to division, representing the varying perceptions of problems that would occur in reality.

Participants work in realistically-arranged offices, complete with telephones and an inter-office post system. They are given an in-tray containing a number of memos, each describing certain issues and problems. Typically 20 participants are involved, and they have between them over 100 problems of varying importance and urgency, many more than can be dealt with in the time available. During the simulation skilled observers watch the proceedings and record the time spent on meetings, paperwork and telephone calls.

The designers claim a high degree of correspondence between behaviour observed within 'Looking Glass' and that found in real managerial jobs. They stress that in order to use the simulation to its full effect, a natural group of managers from a particular company should participate. Intensive debriefing sessions are held after the simulation to ensure that the behaviour of all participants is clarified, and the consequences of the behaviour are clearly discussed and understood. Time is then devoted to relating the lessons back to the real world. Chapter 8 contains some comments of companies that have used Looking Glass for management development purposes.

Financial simulations: risk analysis

The operational simulations described above represent the tangible, physical parts of a system such as a telephone exchange, a factory or a dock. In risk analysis we are only concerned with the financial implications of a particular course of action so the simulations only represent financial data. A typical application of risk analysis is the simulation of an investment decision. As an example, consider that the managers of a particular UK company are considering investing in a European production plant, rather than supplying goods from the UK. There are obviously many important questions to be answered before going ahead.

One of the major questions might be the uncertain demand for the product over the first few years of operation. Because this is partly unknown we express demand not as a single-point estimate as we might for a conventional project appraisal, but as a probability distribution. All of the other major features of the problem will also be represented, again using probability distributions where appropriate, perhaps by little more than educated guesswork at this stage. These features might include future tax rates and exchange rates, and the life of the plant. A model is then constructed representing the appropriate financial calculations.

We now run the simulation and produce the range of results to be expected due to the varying conditions we have specified. The results are, of course, expressed purely in financial terms, and will show standard financial measures of project viability, including, for example, the rate of return on the investment.

After a series of simulations we can build up a picture of how the project rate of return varies. The average rate will be shown, and will usually be the same as would have been obtained from a simple model using single values of sales and costs. However, the simulation will also allow us to study the full range of possible results, from the best to the worst, with associated probabilities. From these we can see what risk we would run of obtaining an unacceptably low rate of return, or perhaps a loss. Hence the term risk analysis.

The method contrasts with conventional methods of project appraisal in which we usually make single estimates of future cash flows, and vary the discount rate in a subjective way to allow for risk. Using the conventional approach we usually obtain artificially accurate single-point answers. Risk analysis is a powerful technique, but it is not an easy one to use. A range of software packages are now available which will carry out the necessary calculations, but the difficulty often lies in the estimation of probability distributions and in the communication of results. An advantage of the method, which partially overcomes this difficulty, is that where a particular assumption is shown to strongly affect the results, then this highlights an issue where we need to take additional advice or care, or perhaps where we must take advance action to ensure the desired result. The technique should never be used to give an automatic decision, or as a substitute for human judgement. Indeed it is best seen as one which allows the implications of that judgement to be assessed. It is above all a technique to provide additional insight into tricky problems.

Simple simulations

Many of the above examples are relatively complex computer-based or manually operated simulations. There are, however, a large number of simple manually operated simulations which rather than representing industrial or other processes, can be used to study a range of individual or social behaviours and events. The content of these is usually very simple and no special briefing or prior knowledge is necessary. The focus in the exercise is usually on the interpersonal or social processes involved, and as a result these exercises are widely accepted as being realistic in many training situations.

They are increasingly used in many different contexts, including school and higher education, and in social services training. The simulations normally use simple equipment, and have few rules. Applications are in time management, teamwork, communications and negotiation skills, supervisor and leadership training.

Self-discovery games

There are a number of games and simulations which are of the 'self-discovery' type. These often put participants in novel situations and encourage them to explore their reactions to these situations. One of these, 'Me- the Slow Learner' (Thatcher and Robinson) is designed to promote empathy for those with learning difficulties. The simulation can be used as an introduction to particular aspects of learning and to how learning can be encouraged or inhibited.

The exercise simulates the effects of impaired vision, poor motor coordination and deafness, and explores the effects of these handicaps on the morale of those involved and their enthusiasm for training. Participants can gain empathy with those who suffer such physical disabilities and an increased ability to develop more suitable training opportunities.

Other simulations have been designed to give participants the experience of moving from one culture to another. Participants work in teams and initially become accustomed to the particular set of rules and the style of working in their own team. After a period of time there is a movement of some individuals between teams, into the 'alien' culture of another team. Participants thus experience at first hand, albeit in a simulated environment, some of the practical and other difficulties of having to adjust to other cultures. This type of exercise would particularly apply to immigrants needing to adjust to the demands of a new country into which they have moved, but can equally be used to illustrate some of the differences between management and shop-floor workers.

Land use games

A number of games have been developed which are suitable for students of land use, planning or social studies, or for anyone needing an insight into the many complex issues that surround decisions in this area. The focus of the game is on how to use a limited amount of land for which there are many competing demands.

Participants work in teams and have to make a number of decisions on how to use the land, including the amount of development they will allow, and for what particular purpose. Background information is provided on the various resources that are available and the competing purposes for which the land could be used.

The simulations are usually manually operated using a number of tables or nomograms. Often maps are provided and different symbols used to show how the particular developments that have been agreed are progressing. Teams can take the differing roles of businesses, schools or housing authorities. The simulations are highly interactive between participants within the same team and between teams.

A particular example is contained in Anderson (1991) in which the Community Land Use Game (CLUG) was used in Mexico for graduate city planning students. CLUG is played on a board and is simple to learn and operate. Participants responded well to the gaming aspects of the exercise and it reinforced the open nature of the land planning process and the need for close interaction between the various parties involved.

Action mazes   An action maze gives participants a particular set of circumstances and then offers a limited set of options. Trainees must choose one option only, as a result of which they are faced with a new set of circumstances which flow from that decision. The trainee is then led to take other decisions, again followed by appropriate results. Mazes are suitable for situations where there is a 'right answer' to the problem and have been used in such areas as health and safety training, counselling and dismissal. Mazes can stimulate a great deal of discussion after the event, and this is best conducted with a trainer skilled in the particular subject area. They can be run manually or can be computer-based.

In-tray exercises   In-tray exercises have been in use for a long time and are best used for training people in specific skills such as time-management or priority setting techniques. Each participant is given a pile of memos or letters, the contents of which should be as close as possible to the real life experience of the trainee. The materials will vary in terms of importance and urgency and the purpose of the exercise is that participants should develop a sensible way of dealing with them. In-tray exercises can require decision-making skills under conditions of considerable pressure.

The exercise has to be adjudicated, usually by a trainer, who will have his own idea of the ideal response to the in-tray problems, but will sometimes have to judge novel solutions which participants have created. In-tray exercises are frequently used for secretarial training for assessing priorities, keeping diaries and mail up to date, and dealing with a variety of customer and staff enquiries.

With the preceding illustrations in mind, we now discuss the general features of all simulations.

Characteristics of simulations

In all simulations, users have a set of goals, implicit or explicit, which they seek to achieve, either in the short or long term. In the case of the flight simulator the trainee's primary goal is to keep the aircraft in a safe condition and on course, whatever the external influences or other occurrences. A secondary goal might be to ensure a comfortable ride for passengers, or to ensure maximum fuel efficiency.

Participants have to pursue these goals by taking action or making a set of decisions. In operational simulations the decisions relate to the acquisition and use of physical resources. In behavioural simulations some of the main decisions might be how participants use their time, and the amount and manner of communication with other participants. Business simulations designed for educational purposes usually involve a number of decisions which are taken at periodic intervals.

In addition there will be a series of constraints or actions that cannot be taken. In the flight simulator there are certain control settings which cannot be exceeded. These will be based upon real-life constraints, so that, for example, the pilot cannot call upon engine power greater than that provided by the particular design of engine. Also he will have to take off at a minimum speed and can only climb at a maximum rate, again determined by the design characteristics of the engine and airframe. Similarly in the Desert Survival exercise, a major constraint is that teams must not split up.

All simulations take place within an environment, which may include other participants or groups involved in the same exercise, who may be hostile or supportive. In the case of the insurance simulation, the environment is provided by the economy modelled by the simulation and by the actions of rival companies in the same business. In the flight simulator the instructor may wish to manipulate the environment to produce a set of unusual conditions rarely met in practice. For example, he or she may wish to see how the trainee deals with an engine failure at takeoff or landing, or how he reacts to an unusual combination of weather conditions and instrument problems.

From the decisions taken and the prevailing environmental conditions, a set of outputs or results will be achieved. These may be good or bad, anticipated or unanticipated. These are among the criteria by which the performance of those participating in the simulation can be judged. We have seen the wide range of results produced by operational simulations. These will be supplemented where appropriate by financial results. Whatever the type of results, it is important that participants are able to relate the results they have achieved to their own actions. In business simulations, the relationship between actions and results can sometimes be clear-cut and sometimes complex. In behavioural simulations it can require considerable skill to understand why things happened how they did, and observers are usually necessary to assist the analysis.

There are various ways that these results can be achieved, sometimes using a model of the real-life situation. We have seen that this can be a physical model or a computer-based model. Business simulations and operational simulations are usually model driven using a computer, and in behavioural simulations, such as Looking Glass, the results are produced by the participants themselves, sometimes with the aid of a referee.

There will also be a degree of predictability of results, according to the conditions the simulation is designed to capture. A random or probabilistic simulation is one in which some or all of the data and relationships vary and are therefore subject to probability distributions. Operational and financial simulations can have by their very nature a high component of unpredictability, and the main reason for using Monte Carlo simulations is their ability to deal explicitly with uncertain events. Behavioural simulations, depending as they do on the responses of the individuals taking part, can also be very unpredictable.

A deterministic simulation is one in which the data and assumptions are known, or assumed in advance, and are not subject to random influences. The simulation is thus no more than a sophisticated set of equations producing a set of results, given the assumptions made. The manpower simulations described above are usually deterministic, as are the more complex simulations based on the insurance company. Business simulations may have both deterministic and probabilistic elements. Table 2.3 summarizes the main features of simulations.

Table 2.3   *Characteristics of simulations*

Purpose	Problem solving	Research	Learning
Decisions	Own decisions	Other decisions	Other influences
Constraints	Rules		Complete freedom
Environment	Bounded by decisions		Influenced by external factors
Production of results	Model-generated	Manually-generated	Produced by participants
Type of results	Operational	Behavioural	Financial
Predictability	Deterministic		Random

Many characteristics of simulations described above can be found in business simulations too. The rapidly changing conditions of commercial and industrial life mean that managers and staff in many organizations need constant training and reorientation to adjust to those changing conditions, in the same way that pilots need to be retrained. Also like pilots, it is the practical on-the-job skills that are essential, and business simulations can provide a very close substitute for that experience. The next chapter discusses business simulations in more detail.

References

Anderson, R. A., 1991 'Simulation in Mexico : A Case Study Using CLUG' in *Simulation and Gaming*, vol. 22, no. 3, pp. 368–72.

Lafferty, J. C. and Pond, A. W., 1986 *The Desert Survival Situation*, Human Synergistics-Verax.

Lombardo, M., McCall, M. and De Vries, D., 1976 *Looking Glass*, Greensboro, NC, Center for Creative Leadership.

Thatcher, D. and Robinson, J., *Solent Simulations*, Fareham, Hampshire.

3 Business simulations in context

The word 'simulation' is sometimes considered too mechanistic for educational purposes, and so the word 'game' is preferred. However, game can imply time-wasting, not taking things too seriously, and engaging in an exercise designed purely for fun. The word 'game' may also conjure up ideas of competition, of rules which must be slavishly obeyed, and strategies devised to confuse the opposition, in ways that may be inappropriate. The term 'gaming simulation' is sometimes used to combine the required features of both games and simulations. From now on in this book the term 'operational simulation' will be used where the purpose is primarily to understand and solve a particular problem, and the term 'business simulation' will be used where the purpose is an educational one.

Although having fun while taking part in a simulation may be important, it is not usually the main purpose of the exercise. In order to stress the educational, rather than the entertainment nature of business simulations, those taking part in the simulation will be described as participants rather than players. Those who run a simulation, whether trainer, teacher or consultant, will be referred to as administrators.

The distinction between operational and business simulations need not be drawn too clearly, since in some ways they serve the same purpose. Business simulations allow people to learn more about various issues that are relevant to part of their business world. Participants can test their ideas in a non-threatening environment rather than in reality and can go some way towards experiencing the results of those ideas. One important difference between the two types of simulation is that in an operational simulation the objective is usually to find the best possible solution to a problem. Business simulations do not usually have this aim, since in reality it is usually impossible to find the best solution to a problem, and this is true even in the simplified world of the simulation.

Another difference is that business simulations always include a range of human behaviour, if only at the aggregate level. This is often represented by the behaviour of buyers, suppliers or competitors who play some part in the simulation. This contrasts for example with the flight simulator, where the pilot is pitted solely against the environment. The pilot knows that although the environment is complex and unpredictable, it is essentially neutral towards him or her. He or she also knows that the laws of aerodynamics can be relied upon; these laws will not be fundamentally changed by the type of aircraft the pilot is flying or by a change in weather conditions.

The possibilities that face the manager in a real business are more complex. For example, an executive in an aircraft design or manufacturing company must be concerned about competing aircraft developed by another firm. It is possible that a new aircraft, while flying no better than existing ones in the aerodynamic sense, will change the commercial rules of the business by being cheaper to produce or more economic to fly. It may introduce a particular new feature which passengers will value, such as the ability to take off and land in a short space, thus allowing the use of airports closer to cities. Business simulations will often therefore incorporate this more complex and less predictable behaviour, whereby one team may change the 'rules of the game' by taking certain actions.

Another difference is that participants in business simulations usually work together in groups. This is deliberate because managers spend so much of business life in groups. Simulations may also involve deliberate role-playing, which can be particularly useful when we ask people to take part in a simulation which focuses on issues which are not part of their normal day-to-day responsibilities.

Some of the many issues that can be addressed by business simulations are as follows:

- the development of fruitful relationships with suppliers and customers
- the development of superior products and services
- teamworking skills
- the coordination of a range of physical and human resources
- the ability to deal with change, risk and uncertainty
- the need to manage within financial or physical constraints
- an understanding of the relationships between different business functions so they may be managed more effectively
- an understanding of how managerial decisions effect financial results
- the construction and analysis of financial statements
- an understanding of what makes for success in different markets, countries and cultures

How business simulations differ

Table 3.1 on p. 25 shows some of the main ways in which business simulations differ.

Production of results

All simulations need ways to produce the results of participants' actions. Sometimes this is done manually, using some type of chart or nomogram. Some simulations require judges to assess performance. In the case of computer-based simulations, the computer model will itself calculate most but not necessarily all of the results.

As an example, let us consider a simple simulation involving the sale of

Table 3.1 *How business simulations differ*

Production of results	Computer Quantitative	Manual Scenario-driven
Interactions	Independence	Full interaction
Participants	Individuals Junior staff	Teams Senior managers
Focus	Functional	Corporate
Timescale	Tactical	Strategic
Scope	National	International
Type of results	Operations Printed	Functional Graphical
Decision aids	Part of the simulation	Separate

one product, the demand for which might potentially be influenced by two variables. For simplicity we will assume these are the expenditure on advertising in a local newspaper, and the selling price of the product. These might be among several decisions that teams have to make at periodic intervals. Figure 3.1 shows a possible relationship between the amount of money spent on local advertising and sales of the product. The line starts at zero where none of the potential customers are aware of the product, and increases steadily as the amount of advertising increases.

Note that the effectiveness of the advertising begins to decrease after certain levels of expenditure have been exceeded. This could occur for a number of reasons, including the possibility that readers of the newspaper might become bored with the advertisement and begin to ignore it. Note also that no matter how great the advertising, not all potential

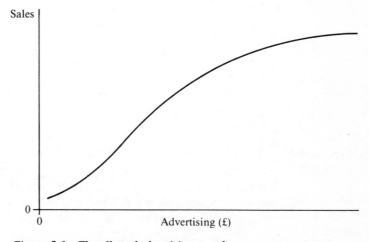

Figure 3.1 *The effect of advertising on sales*

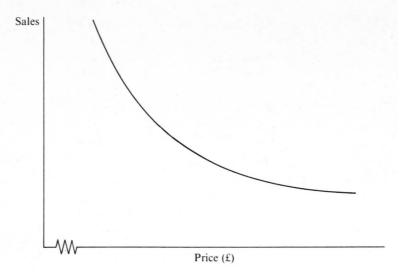

Figure 3.2   *The effect of price on sales*

customers will buy the product, for the simple reason that not everyone reads the newspaper, or perhaps they feel no need for the product or find a more suitable one elsewhere. Potential customers might also be influenced by the price of the product. Figure 3.2 shows how selling price might affect sales.

It might be hard to establish the appropriate form of these two curves and in reality the situation would be even more complex, with several variables all having an impact on sales. In this simple example we could suppose a combined effect derived from the multiplication of price effect and advertising effect. The nomogram shown in Figure 3.3 shows how the combined effects of the two variables could be displayed. Chapter 5 shows how these relationships may be constructed in a simple form during the design of an actual simulation.

So even to show the combined effect of these two relatively simple variables requires a fairly complex graphical approach. It will be appreciated just how long it could take to read off several values from such a nomogram. When more variables and more products are involved the task becomes almost impossible. However, the combined results can be obtained very simply using a model within a computer program. For this reason most business simulations use a computer model of the business situation to produce results.

Model-based simulations

The above example of the combined effects of two variables may be modelled very easily using a single equation, thus replacing the nomogram or other manual methods. The model can also be extended to include other variables and the interactions between competitors. At the simplest level, therefore, models contain inputs, outputs and a means of translating inputs into outputs, as shown in Figure 3.4.

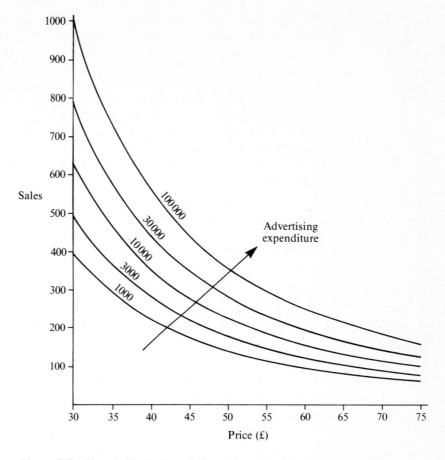

Figure 3.3 *The combined effect of advertising and price on sales*

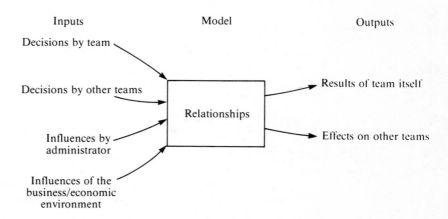

Figure 3.4 *A model*

It is important to realize that the model is merely a creation of the person or team who designed it. It represents the designers' opinions of how the real world (or part of it) behaves. In a business simulation the model translates the action of the participant(s) and any other inputs into tangible results. In the example of the flight simulator described in Chapter 2 the model was contained within complex computer software which translates all inputs (actions by the pilot, conditions of the environment and influences by the instructor) into overall flight conditions and instrument readings. Clearly, the models used are of a very high order of complexity, and by comparison the models underlying business simulations are relatively simple.

In essence, therefore, the model contains a number of cause and effect relationships. It is worth while pointing out at this stage that any model is the result of considerable research and deliberation. The flight simulator is developed after extensive study of the design characteristics of the aircraft. These are then represented in the software which is intended to produce results appropriate to any prevailing conditions. Even the comparatively simple models used in business simulations are often the result of a considerable period of research by the designers, and in the case of a tailor-made simulation, by the organization for whom the simulation is intended. The model will accept a number of quantitative decisions, and will process these to produce a series of quantitative results. This is not to say that computer-based models only feature quantitative issues. As will be seen later there are ways that many equally important qualitative activities can be involved in simulations.

One advantage of computer-based simulations is the flexibility of decision values. For example, in a simulation involving pricing decisions, prices can be expressed as accurately as required, to the nearest pound or penny. Results will be produced just as easily, whatever values of price are required. In a manual simulation, however, approximations often have to be made.

The production of results can be a complex enough process when each decision variable acts independently, but in reality this is seldom the case. For example, in a marketing simulation, the 'four Ps' of position, promotion, price and product features will all interact. This introduces two problems; one is to agree what those interactions are, and the second is to devise a method to show the appropriate results of any combination of decision values. There are a number of ways of producing a nomogram to achieve this manually, but the process quickly becomes very unwieldy. On the other hand, a computer program can handle any number of decision variables.

Computer-based simulations have the added advantage that they can produce results quickly, accurately and objectively. Any relationship that can be represented logically, pictorially or algebraically can be included in a computer program, and the program can allow the kind of relationships which would be very difficult to express in other ways. Also the program can handle any inadmissible decision values automatically, by checking at the input stage and applying suitable amendments if necessary.

A practical advantage is that the computer program leaves administrators free to focus on other important aspects of the simulation. As many copies of output as are required may be produced, and the program can be designed to provide a number of forecasting and 'what if?' modelling facilities. Chance events may also be easily designed into the program. Simulations that repeat the same set of decisions over several time periods can become tedious after a while and another option is to introduce additional decisions from time to time as the situation unfolds. These are sometimes called 'progressive' games, and are much easier if computer-based.

Another advantage is that the computer can be used to make as much or as little information available as is appropriate, and the information can be presented in different ways. The time involved in doing this would usually be prohibitive in a manual simulation. So taken in conjunction with the increasing availability of small cheap computers, the case for computer-based simulations becomes very strong.

One disadvantage of computer-based simulations is that it is possible to focus on the technology rather than the main educational purpose of the simulation. Computer-based simulations demand an increased range of skills from the administrator. They can also make life too easy for participants, for example if they do not have to work through their accounts to understand how they achieved their present position. However, it is not necessary for the computer program to produce all the required results. If, for example, one of the purposes of the simulation is to encourage participants to create their own accounts in order to fully understand the financial consequences of their actions, then it is a simple matter to design the simulation so that it produces part of the results only, leaving the accounts to be produced manually.

Whether manual or computer-based, the simulation administrator has to understand how results relate to all the decisions made. With computer-based simulations there can be a tendency to build in additional complex relationships merely because it is easy to do so. The relationships in the computer program can indeed be so complex that they become opaque to all but the simulation designer.

Another type of simulation is the 'scenario based' simulation. Here participants are presented with a number of scenarios at regular intervals, each chosen to typify the kind of problems that occur in the industry or activity represented in the simulation. Participants are offered several courses of action and have to choose what they believe to be the most appropriate one. These simulations contain a model which shows how the various courses of action affect the results or output variables. The simulation will, therefore, react in appropriate ways according to the course of action chosen, for example to show the effect on staff morale or product quality. The models are ideally research-based to ensure that appropriate relationships are used.

Interactions Two types of interaction are possible in simulations, model-based interaction and human interaction. Model-based interaction means the extent
to which one team's results are dependent on their own decisions, or
the decisions of other teams. The best example of this is in the calculation of one team's market share of a product or service. To what extent
will the team's market share depend on their own marketing decisions,
i.e. pricing and advertising, and how much will it depend on other
teams' decisions? Any required degree of model-based interaction may
be introduced between teams, ranging from the complete isolation of
teams one from another, to complete interaction. The latter represents a
perfect market in which one team only gains an additional customer at
the expense of another team. The second type of interaction is between
participants and refers to a variety of face-to-face contacts that take place
between individuals and teams in the course of the simulation.

Participants Participants can be at any level of seniority and possess any level of
expertise, from undergraduates or new entrants to senior managers,
providing the simulation is designed appropriately. They can act as individuals if required, or more likely they will need to work in teams.
Many simulations are too complex for one person to handle well in a
given timescale, thus interaction will occur quite naturally, both within
the members of one team, and between different teams. The amount of
interaction will, however, be strongly influenced by the design of the
simulation. Sometimes participants can be grouped into teams representing different levels within the hierarchy of an organization, for
example the board and an operating unit. This might well introduce
some of the communication difficulties that occur in real organizations.

Focus The focus of a simulation can either be on the activities of one or more
departments or functions in an organization, or on the organization as a
whole. In the case of a simulation dealing with the manufacturing part
of a company, the concerns might be on production volume, timing and
quality, and perhaps on related issues such as productivity, training,
recruitment, or the acquisition of appropriate materials and other
resources. In the case of a simulation dealing with broader corporate
issues there would normally be less detail within each department or
part of the business, and a range of strategic issues would be included.
These might concern not only production, but marketing and distribution,
purchasing, design and financial matters, and broader employee and
shareholder concerns. The focus will depend on the learning aims and
participants' current functional knowledge or general management
awareness.

Timescale The most appropriate timescale can be chosen according to the overall
purpose and scope of the simulation. Typical decision periods might be
a month, a quarter or a year, and the simulation could last between six
and twelve periods. Where seasonality is a major feature of the business
then obviously annual decision periods are inappropriate and shorter time
periods must be used. Alternatively, if the purpose is to stress the need for

long-term planning then six monthly or annual periods might be appropriate.

Scope The operations depicted within the simulation can be wholly contained within national boundaries, or they can span several countries. If more than one country is concerned then additional complexities are involved, for example there might be several different exchange and inflation rates. Some European simulations use the ECU as a measure of currency, partly to overcome this problem. The complexities involved in modelling multinational operations are considerable, but the results can be very worth while. Simulations can be built around almost any industry, manufacturing, retail, distribution, service or utility, but manufacturing backgrounds are most popular since they are the easiest to model. There are also a growing number of simulations that focus on issues other than purely business ones, for example social and environmental topics.

Type of results Results can be expressed in purely operational terms, for example the numbers of orders received, sales made, or employees hired, or in financial terms too. It is usually an easy matter to allow the model to calculate the financial results of operational decisions in as much detail as required. Most simulations produce printed results, especially where these are required to conform to particular financial reporting practices. Commercially available simulations often produce results in graphical form too, sometimes in great variety.

Decision aids Computer-based simulations are ideally suited to the provision of decision aids. These can provide a means of forecasting the demand for the product or service represented in the simulation, or enable participants to carry out financial analyses before making decisions. The aids can be provided as part of the simulation software or as separate features. Sometimes it might be part of the purpose of the simulation to encourage participants to develop their own decision aids.

Complexity and reality No simulation can ever be totally realistic, no matter how complex it is. Complexity is not a substitute for reality, and in any case reality is as much a subjective matter, within the mind of the participants, as it is an objective matter connected with the number of equations in the simulation model, or the amount of detail used in the representation of production or financial issues. The most important thing is the extent to which participants believe the simulation to be a valid activity. In some ways the lack of total reality in a simulation is an advantage. Reality is full of insignificant issues as well as important ones, and it is the designer's job to distil from reality the issues which are critical to the purpose of the simulation. So a degree of 'designed-in unreality' might be deliberate and useful. The extreme complexity of some commercial simulations might in some cases be due as much to the background of the simulation designer as to the needs of intended participants. Our concern is for educational simulations which focus on a number of topics relevant to participants, in order to develop their understanding or improve their skills. If we are in doubt about the appropriate degree of complexity it is useful to ask a number of questions about the purpose of the simulation, the intended audience, their current knowledge and what they are required to learn. To help in this process Chapter 4 deals with the vital issue of how adults learn, and the part played by simulations and other learning methods in that process.

Research into the practical uses of simulations

Many attempts have been made to find how business simulations have been used in practice, mainly in the USA and to a lesser extent in the UK. Horn and Cleaves found that over 200 business simulations were in use among a total of over 1200 manual and computer-based simulations in the USA (Horn and Cleaves, 1981). Several researchers in the USA have surveyed the views of simulation users in business and in universities. Faria (1987) found that 95 per cent of business schools used business games, and that they were most frequently used in business policy and marketing faculties. They were used more extensively at the undergraduate level than at the graduate level. Business school deans rated business simulations more highly than business school teachers (as they did all methods with the exception of lectures).

Over half of US companies have been found to use some form of simulation game or exercise for initial and ongoing training programmes (Faria, 1987). Users ranged from trainees to top managers. Most used simulations developed outside the organization, and were manually operated.

Burgess (1991) studied business simulations used among higher education establishments, professional institutions and large companies in the UK. Among the educational establishments, simulations were used most for post-experience courses. There was equal usage of games purchased from outside suppliers and those developed in-house.

Both Faria and Burgess showed that simulations were widely used in academic establishments, but less so in industry. Jacobs (1987) supported this and found it surprising since, as discussed in Chapter 4, simulations comply with adult learning theory. When questioned about their views on the future use of simulations, most users expected the usage of simulations to either stay at the same level or increase over the next two years. There appears to be a higher rate of usage of simulations in the USA than in the UK, but this might be partly due to the fact that Faria included non computer-based simulations while Burgess only included computer-based ones. In academic circles, however, the usages were both over 90 per cent.

McKenna (1991) reported on the experiences of using business simulations in Australian universities and colleges. The use of business simulations had increased rapidly over the last few years, but usage was still some way behind the levels found in the USA. Of the 18 simulations described, only two were Australian, the rest being from the USA. Users rated simulations rather more highly than other teaching methods. McKenna made the comment that simulations developed in the USA were not necessarily appropriate in Australia, due possibly to differing business and economic conditions in the two countries. For example, Australia's population and the size of its manufacturing sector are both much smaller in scale.

Pros and cons of business simulations

A limitation of much of the work described above is its concentration on the extent to which simulations are used under particular circumstances. Very little has been found out about the reasons why simulations are used or not used, and the opinions of users on their merits or disadvantages as learning methods. Therefore, in late 1991 the author asked about 150 managers and others working in management development about their views on business simulations as methods of management training and development.

A short questionnaire was sent to management development and training managers, and to others involved in training in the UK. Replies were received from individuals representing organizations of all sizes and types, from management consultancies, training colleges, banks and insurance companies, chemical and oil companies, utilities and leisure organizations, retailers, office suppliers and aerospace manufacturers.

Forty-six replies were received (representing around 32 per cent of the sample) and the results are summarized below. A 32 per cent response rate is quite good for this type of questionnaire, but due to the small number of replies the results must be treated with caution. Nevertheless, the results are illuminating and show a high regard for games and simulations, but suggest a number of reservations and possible improvements.

Most respondents were employed in small- or medium-sized organizations, 60 per cent stating that there were less than 300 managers in their organizations. Twenty-two per cent had between 300 and 3000 managers, and 18 per cent had over 3000 managers.

Simulations had obviously been used to a varying extent. At the extremes, 59 per cent of respondents had used simulations four or more times over the last year, and 15 per cent had not used simulations at all. The latter percentage must be treated with caution since there is naturally a danger of a biased response to the questionnaire. Those who do not use simulations or who are less enthusiastic about them may be less likely to reply than those who are users or who are more enthusiastic. On the other hand, it could be argued that only those who have used simulations are really aware of their benefits and limitations, and therefore only they are qualified to express an opinion. Non-users gave a number of reasons why they did not use simulations. Several thought that simulations were not appropriate to their particular situation, or they knew of no suitable ones or felt they did not have sufficient expertise to run it.

Most simulations were computer-based and had been obtained almost equally frequently from three sources—'off-the-shelf' from a supplier, tailor-made by a supplier, or developed in-company. Simulations were almost always used as part of training courses and were thought to be most effective when integrated with other material, including lectures, discussions and case studies. They were thought to be rather more applicable for middle and senior managers than for junior managers or supervisors.

Benefits of simulations

Respondents were asked what specific benefits they found in using simulations. Several potential benefits were offered, and each was scored on the scale; 1 (very useful), 2 (moderately useful), 3 (of little use) or 4 (of no use). The results were as follows:

Benefit	*Mean score*
To help participants understand how different areas of the business interrelate	1.3
For team-building purposes	1.3
To develop decision-making skills	1.6
To develop marketing knowledge and skill	1.7
To give participants a better insight into other areas of the business	1.7
To develop financial knowledge and skill	1.7

Respondents were asked more generally about their views on the advantages of simulations and these are grouped under the following headings.

Motivation

Many people said the enjoyment and 'fun' aspects of simulations were important and felt that the main reason for this was that simulations were highly participative and interactive. The element of competition was thought to be beneficial, often leading to a high level of commitment. Many participants found that taking part in a simulation was a truly memorable learning experience.

Teamworking

The development of teamworking skills was among the strongest benefit of simulations, as shown above. The simulation often led to the formation of cohesive teams, and could be a valid method to explore team roles (in the 'Belbin' sense). Simulations could demonstrate that for effective team performance, participants must clarify their roles and yet be prepared to be flexible and not adhere to that role too rigidly. Simulations could also lead to the development of a common business 'language and understanding' which could be shared among the team. This advantage was particularly useful when participants came from the same organization or department.

A risk-free environment

The most frequently mentioned advantage was that simulations offered a comparatively 'risk-free environment', and therefore encouraged participants to act creatively and experiment with a variety of different behaviours. This was an opportunity not encountered at work. Simulations could also compress a lengthy timespan of business activity in a short period and the experience was thought to give participants the added confidence necessary to get involved in other areas of the business.

Variety Simulations brought a welcome change of pace and variety in training courses. They were thought to be most useful when combined with other learning activities, including behavioural training. They could have a valuable 'ice breaking' role at the start of a training course and they could also give a good general awareness of a range of managerial skills, including influencing and decision-making skills, negotiation and leadership. One of their main uses was in integrating all the various aspects of the business in a way that gave a useful overall view of the organization.

An 'experiential' learning method Many managers said that simulations provided participants with quick and unambiguous feedback of results, enabling them to see the consequences of their actions very clearly in 'three dimensions'. Frequently, these consequences could be apparent in a number of ways, for example from the financial, human resource, market and customer points of view. This comment is closely related to the main advantage shown above, that simulations gave participants an insight into the way that different areas of the business interrelate. Thus simulations can offer participants the opportunity for insight not available in other ways. Some respondents expressed these advantages in another way by saying that simulations used more phases of the Kolb learning cycle than most other learning methods.

Realism Many felt that simulations were realistic, particularly if tailor-made for a particular organization or situation. They could represent any desired features of a particular industry and offer a good approximation of the type of skills that many managers needed to be successful.

Disadvantages of simulations Respondents were asked about the limitations of simulations and these are summarized below.

They are 'just a game'? A minority of respondents found simulations artificial and unrealistic. Some felt that the 'game' element was sometimes over-emphasized and that participants could concentrate too much on 'winning the game' or 'beating the computer', rather than taking the exercise seriously and reflecting on the lessons it offered.

Complexity Simulations could be too complex and time-consuming for some respondents, and several stressed the need for a competent and well-prepared person to run them. Complex simulations required a fairly high degree of computer literacy, and it could be difficult to run the simulation, respond to participants' requests, and keep an overall view of what was happening in the simulation. The latter was particularly necessary for the debriefing session. This clearly underlines the importance of debriefing put forward in Chapter 7.

'Not suitable for us' A few people felt that the most important aspects of business life were the hardest to quantify, and therefore they could not be included in simulations. Several people expressed the concern that there were no simulations suitable for their particular company or circumstances.

Cost-effectiveness One question addressed the issue of cost-effectiveness. Respondents were asked the extent to which they thought that simulations represented value for money, relative to other training and development methods. The options were 'very good value for money', 'moderately good value for money', 'little value' and 'poor value'. Only users were able to answer this question.

A surprising 41 per cent of respondents described simulations as very good value for money and 49 per cent thought they were moderately good value. This result suggests that even though simulations can be time-consuming and expensive, 90 per cent of users thought they were good value for money. This result compares with Burgess's finding that nearly 90 per cent of business simulation users found them 'extremely useful' or 'moderately useful'.

Suggested developments The last point was amplified when participants were asked what developments they would like to see in simulations in order to make them more appropriate or effective.

Customization Many comments revolved around the extent to which simulations were appropriate to the circumstances of the intended participants. Many felt that simulations were most effective when tailor-made. Several respondents suggested that simulations should use company data and more closely reflect the market and economic environment and structure of the particular organization in which it is used. Several also mentioned the difficulty of finding suitable custom-built products, and suggested a number of ways of overcoming this, including the development of more tailor-made products (especially for service industries), or the design of standard products in modular form so that they could be easily adapted for any particular use.

Ease of use It was thought vital that simulations were simple in design and that they focused on the main learning purposes. Many thought that simulations were not easy to use at the moment, and there was a plea for the 'information technology' element to be as unobtrusive as possible.

A missed opportunity? Several respondents mentioned that there were missed opportunities in using simulations. In particular, it was thought that an individual suitably trained in organizational behaviour could provide useful insights and feedback into individual and group behaviour exhibited during the simulation. When used as part of a course, simulations could be more closely interwoven with other subjects covered on the course, requiring the simulation to be highly tailored. Simulations could also inject random or unexpected events, thus testing participants' ability to respond quickly and flexibly to novel circumstances.

Conclusions

Many educational establishments and household-name companies in the USA, the UK and elsewhere now use business simulations as a routine way of educating managers and others. There is still doubt in some quarters about their educational effectiveness compared with other learning methods, but on the whole the evidence suggests that simulations are at least as good, and in many cases better than other methods. The next chapter will address the subject of adult learning and the part played by simulations.

References

Burgess, T. F., June 1991 'The Use of Computerised Management and Business Games in the United Kingdom', in *Simulation and Gaming*, vol. 22, no. 2, pp. 174–95.

Faria, A. J., June 1987 'A Survey of the Use of Business Games in Academia and Business', in *Simulation and Games*, vol. 18, no. 2, pp. 207–24.

Horn, R. E. and Cleaves, A., 1980 *The Guide to Simulation/Games for Education and Training*, Sage, California.

Jacobs, R. L. and Baum, M., September 1987 'Simulation and Games in Training and Development', in *Simulation and Games*, vol. 18, no. 3, pp. 385–94.

McKenna, R. J., March 1991 'Business Computerized Simulation: The Australian Experience', in *Simulation and Games*, vol. 22, no. 1, pp. 36–62.

4 Approaches to learning

Many people find that their most important period of learning was at school or college. Here the teacher or lecturer was the expert, and the methods used were mainly based upon lectures, textbooks and exercises of various kinds. There is also a natural tendency to believe that once school or college is over, learning is finished and life can begin. There is nothing further to learn, or that needs to be learned from life itself, since learning and doing are mutually incompatible activities.

Yet in today's rapidly changing world this can hardly be true any longer. World events and business life are changing so fast that the ability to learn and adapt to new circumstances is vital. Previously learned knowledge and skills can quickly become obsolete, and there is a clear need to continually learn and relearn new knowledge and new skills. This is particularly true of managers who may change jobs or even careers several times during their working lives. Many have to face difficult challenges which formal school or college education has not prepared them for. This puts a high premium on their ability to learn.

The focus in both academic and practical business circles is increasingly on learning. For example, IBM has stated that its business is learning, and that it sells the products of that learning. The renewed interest in learning is also shown in the debate about the Learning Organization. This has been defined as an organization that encourages the learning of all its employees, and thereby continually transforms itself as its environment changes. However the Learning Organization is defined, individual members of the organization are clearly the key to the learning process. Garratt has described learning as 'a key process of survival and development in a business' (Garratt, 1987, p. 61).

If companies' most worthwhile assets are their employees, then those assets must be kept up-to-date just as physical assets are maintained and updated. This involves the creation of circumstances in which people can learn, not on a once-off or occasional basis, but continually, and by doing this an organization can acquire its most enduring competitive edge. We now examine some recent ideas on how people learn.

How do managers learn?

It is useful to distinguish between three types of managerial learning: cerebral learning, skills learning and what has been called transformational learning (Bateson, 1973). Cerebral learning is the acquisition of new factual information and knowledge which is of direct relevance to the manager. A good example is learning specific professional or functional knowledge about the business, or general knowledge about the industry in which the manager works. However, no matter how essential cerebral learning might be, it is not much good unless it results in more effective behaviour.

Skills learning builds upon cerebral learning and results in observable changes in behaviour. The acquisition of a particular social skill, such as interviewing skills, is a good example of this type of learning. The skills thus acquired are often more transferable from one situation to another than cerebral learning.

Transformational learning occurs when learners become aware of their view of how the world works, and of the learning that is taking place within them. This type of learning is often more personal and can have a profound effect on individuals, leading to improvements in the way they handle a wide range of situations. People exhibit this type of learning when they change their 'theory in use', or their understanding of the way the world works, in response to experience or new insights. This happens when they make their theory in use explicit, and compare it with the understanding of others and with the evidence of the world around them. This will allow the creation of more effective theories.

Kelly made a similar point when he said that people make sense of the world about them by continually structuring and restructuring it. People make implicit assumptions about the reality they experience and subsequently find out how useful these assumptions are in anticipating events. In Kelly's view these assumptions take the form of bipolar constructs, which are organized into hierarchical construct systems. As people experience the world they can reorganize their constructs (their 'theory in use'). Events can be classified in different ways, or constructs can be discarded or elaborated (Kelly, 1955).

Learning is thus not merely the acquisition of new knowledge or skill, but the reorganization of what is already known. The speed and effectiveness of learning will therefore depend strongly on the way in which new information is presented and organized for the learner. This kind of learning and relearning is clearly the most appropriate for managers in today's world. A crucial feature of the self-aware learner is thus the ability to evaluate one's own knowledge and performance and bring one's own learning processes under review.

The actual process of learning is often described as one involving a series of steps, rather than as a discreet event. It is often shown as a cyclical process in which a new experience is followed by other activities which help to make sense of that experience. As a result of these activities comes new understanding or ability which can then be put into practice. The process involves not only absorbing new experiences, but constantly changing our existing skills and attitudes and relating them to existing knowledge. Kolb described this process in his four-stage model of experiential learning as shown in Figure 4.1 (Kolb *et al*, 1991, p. 59).

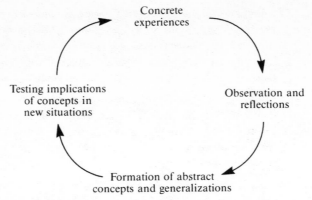

Figure 4.1   The experiential learning model (reprinted with permission from David A. Kolb, Irwin M. Rubin and Joyce M. Osland, *Organizational Behaviour: An Experiential Approach*, 5th edition, 1991, p. 59, Prentice Hall, Englewood Cliffs, New Jersey)

Kolb suggests that learning is an integrated process involving here-and-now experience, followed by a period of observation and reflection on that experience. This in turn will lead to clearer understanding of the situation in the form of generalizations and abstract concepts, leading to a new theory about the way that part of the world works. The new theory is no good in itself, however, and will only be useful if it leads to new ideas for action. These actions are finally tested out in practice and new experience gained. The four stages are called concrete experience (CE), reflective observation (RO), abstract conceptualization (AC) and active experimentation (AE).

We clearly need to develop an ability in all four of these phases, yet some of them are apparently contradictory. As Kolb states 'How can one act and reflect at the same time? How can one be concrete and immediate and still be theoretical?' (Kolb, 1976, p. 22). People tend to develop stronger abilities in some of these activities than in others, partly as a result of heredity and partly due to life experiences. This leads to the concept of a learning 'style' and Kolb gives a number of examples. Mathematicians value the ability to develop abstract concepts, poets thrive on concrete experience, naturalists develop good observational skills, or managers might be most oriented towards the practical application of ideas (Kolb, 1976, p. 23).

It therefore follows that people with different learning styles often prefer to learn things in different ways, and this can have a profound influence on the design of learning events. There may be a deliberate attempt to develop the less-used and less-preferred learning skills, thus enhancing the all-round style, and at other times there may be an attempt to further improve an already well-developed learning skill.

The learning cycle happens all the time in all human activity, although often unconsciously. Kolb points out that the most effective learner is one who can develop abilities in all four of these stages. The best learning methods will allow learners to apply their previous knowledge of a subject to a new situation, and hence acquire new experience. In order to maximize the benefit of that experience, however, learners must have the opportunity to stand back from the experience and reflect on it. This in turn will lead to new insights, and a set of new or altered concepts. Learners will not always form the most appropriate 'theory in use', however, especially when dealing with new material. The trainer will need to provide help by suggesting new models and theories which others have found useful. These newly-acquired concepts or theoretical understanding of the problem are no good in their own right. They must lead people to try out new behaviour or approaches, in other words to experiment. This leads us back to where we started, to gaining new experience.

Honey and Mumford considerably extended the Kolb model of experience-based learning. They developed an 80-question Learning Style Questionnaire (LSQ) which approaches the question of learning by describing a range of managerial activities. They present a practical workbook which allows managers to understand work on their own learning style. Their *Manual of Learning Styles* (1992) includes the LSQ itself and discusses learning as a highly personal process and as a continuous one. It shows how trainers can use the LSQ to adopt more appropriate learning experiences. It also includes LSQ norms for various occupational groups.

This supplements an earlier publication, also based on the LSQ (Honey and Mumford, 1986). The earlier work can be used by learners to choose learning activities that suit particular learning styles, or supplement under-developed ones.

The Honey and Mumford learning styles are very similar to those outlined by Kolb and are called the Activist, Reflector, Theorist and Pragmatist. The experience-based approach can thus claim to have received substantial support, and is the basis for a wide range of learning events.

For any learning event to be successful, it is vital that learners give it their full and willing cooperation. In some circumstances learners may see little immediate need to learn, or little apparent relevance of the subject. For people to learn most effectively, the subject matter must therefore either have intrinsic interest to them, or they will need to have their interest stimulated in some way. This interest can be aroused either by the individual coming to realize his or her need for knowledge of a subject, perhaps by discovering his or her comparative ignorance, or perhaps by coming into contact with someone who inspires further interest. This is one of the key roles of the trainer or lecturer. It can, however, be a painful experience for some people, since it may need an admission that they are not as expert in a subject as they had previously believed, possibly requiring some 'unlearning' if their 'theory in use' was clearly wrong.

The experiential approach emphasizes that learning is maximized when the individual learner is fully involved in the learning event. The event should evoke a full range of emotional, intellectual and practical responses, and the skilled trainer will help to ensure this happens. In order to take action and test out their new understanding, particularly when developing new skills, learners need to feel sure that no one is going to criticize or laugh at them. Learning is, therefore, likely to be most effective when it takes place in a non-threatening environment. It is not always possible for people to try out new ideas or practise new behaviour in the real working situation, or in the presence of those who will be too judgemental when observing their behaviour. So the need can arise for an artificial learning exercise which takes place off the job.

Whatever learning methods are being used, there is also the need for sufficient time for the lessons of the exercise to be fully absorbed. People will need time to inwardly digest what has happened and make sense of it, as Kolb states in the abstract conceptualization stage of his model. Again the period of reflection and generalization should be an integral part of the learning event, facilitated where appropriate by the trainer.

There is also the question of how much skill or knowledge in a subject a particular individual needs to acquire, which will depend on his or her personal circumstances. There may just be the need for the illustration of a particular issue, purely at the awareness level, with no need to impart any deep understanding or personal skill. Alternatively, the learner might wish to acquire a deeper understanding or need to acquire skill in a particular area so that he or she can exhibit the new learning in practical ways. This can take place at several levels, culminating in the degree of expertise which enables the learner to demonstrate by appropriate behaviour that he or she has acquired a high degree of skill in the subject.

Taking account of the insight provided by the experiential learning model, and the practical arguments presented above, we now propose an extended model of the learning process, as shown in Figure 4.2. The trainer has a vital role in several stages of the model, in providing an insight into and enthusiasm for the subject, explaining the subject area, ensuring that the learning takes place in a non-threatening environment, helping people to reflect on what they have experienced, and where appropriate, giving new theoretical inputs and frameworks. These roles are shown in Figure 4.2.

What do managers need to learn?

Having discussed how managers learn, and the conditions under which they learn best, we now turn to the question of what they need to learn. It is, of course, not possible to generalize too far, as the content will depend largely on the situation that the manager is in and his or her abilities and knowledge at any point in time. Indeed a period of diagnosis will often be necessary before the learning event can be designed. This question relates to the competence issue about which there has been a great deal of debate over the last few years. The debate has centred around several questions, including whether there is a generally agreed set of knowledge, skills and attitudes (competences) that are necessary for

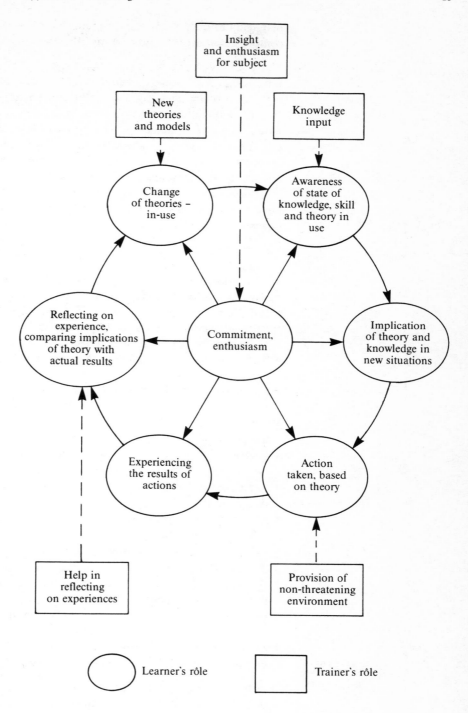

Figure 4.2 *How we learn*

managers to operate successfully, and the extent to which any such set of competences can be valid in a rapidly changing world (Woodruffe, 1991).

Many different sets of competences have been published, all differing in the precise terminology used and in the way that they have been clustered into recognizable groups. Without wishing to enter into the debate about the usefulness of competences, let us say that they do at least provide a reasonably objective starting point for management development and training activities, although the relative importance of any one competence will naturally depend on the particular situation. The following list is a simplified one from a variety of sources and will be used to compare various learning methods. In practice the competences would need to be specified in practical detail and in observable behavioural terms.

- *Basic facts and knowledge*: about the company, industry or the world at large.
- *Sensitivity to events*: in order to be able to interpret events in the outside world and act appropriately.
- *Self-awareness*: the ability to know one's own strengths and limitations.
- *Personal effectiveness*: for example the ability to use time wisely, and to set and meet personal objectives.
- *Teamworking and teambuilding skills*: the ability to create, work as part of, or manage a team.
- *Leadership skills*: the ability to take charge where necessary and get results.
- *Social and communication skills*: among the most important set of skills for all managers.
- *Emotional resilience*: the ability and toughness to keep on trying, and not to be put off by difficulties or setbacks.
- *Creativity*: the attitude and ability to find new and better ways of doing things.
- *Mental and intellectual skills*: to deal with information, grasp facts and inferences and solve problems.
- *Balanced learning habits*: the all-round learning skills necessary to maximize learning.
- *Ability to deal with change*: flexibility and adaptability in the face of an ever-changing world.
- *Willingness to take risks*: the attitude which allows individuals to act on partial information and to risk being wrong.
- *Knowing the big picture*: vision, awareness of the strategy of the organization and how this is derived—the ability to impart this to others.

A similar set of qualities for successful managers can be found in Pedler *et al* (1986), together with self-diagnostic tools and a range of appropriate self-development activities.

Learning methods

There has undoubtedly been a shift in recent years from traditional learning methods towards more practical and experience-based ones. Managers are becoming less satisfied with traditional lectures and other one-way learning methods. They demand a wider range of activities, particularly those which offer practical involvement. These types of activity are much closer to the everyday world of the manager, who by the nature of the managerial job, is largely action-oriented.

The need to make methods more practical applies equally to all of the three types of learning outlined above. For example, those providing cerebral learning would be providing knowledge input, but to ensure the knowledge has really been learned, some degree of practice is essential. Skill-developing learning clearly cannot take place without offering an opportunity to practise those skills. Transformational learning would also need the learner to be able to be involved in each phase of the learning cycle, particularly in reflective observation and abstract conceptualization.

Apart from the more theoretical arguments presented above, there are practical reasons to believe that the kind of model of the learning process presented in Figure 4.2 is useful. Nevertheless, there are still many occasions when the lecturer or textbook (or its modern equivalent) may well be the most appropriate learning method. We now compare some of the most popular learning methods in use in management development and training. Table 4.1 shows which of the various learning methods described here contribute most to the list of competences outlined above.

Learning on the job

Many managers are becoming aware that work itself, if seen in an appropriate light, can become a means of learning. One of the recurring complaints about off-the-job learning is its relevance to work. In fact, to many people this 'learning by doing' is the most natural method of learning, and learning on the job will remain the main learning method for many managers. Managers have among their responsibilities the duty to see that their own abilities, and those of their staff, are developed as fully as possible. Managers can ensure that on-the-job learning happens for others by creating an appropriate environment and atmosphere at work and by offering practical help and insights. The maximum learning benefit will only occur if adequate opportunities are provided to reflect on experiences in a deliberate way.

Action learning

Action learning is a method of management development in which managers are required to face and solve real organizational problems for which there is no known answer. The task is not just to study or theorize about problems, but to take action to solve them.

Each manager involved in action learning usually has another manager in the organization, who is the client who 'owns' the problem, and who will help to provide access to information and people in order to solve it. Action learning typically involves people working in action learning 'sets'. These are groups of managers, all working on different problems, who come together periodically for discussion and mutual support. The sets often have a facilitator whose job it is to ensure that the set

	Learning on the job	Action learning	Coaching and counselling	Resource centre learning	Business simulations	Outdoor management development	Case studies	Lectures
Basic facts and knowledge				✔	✔		✔	✔
Sensitivity to events	✔	✔	✔			✔		
Self-awareness		✔	✔		✔	✔		
Personal effectiveness		✔	✔	✔				✔
Teamworking	✔	✔	✔		✔	✔		✔
Leadership	✔	✔				✔		
Social and communication skills	✔		✔		✔	✔	✔	
Emotional resilience	✔	✔	✔			✔		
Creativity		✔	✔				✔	✔
Mental agility			✔	✔	✔		✔	✔
Balanced learning habits		✔	✔		✔			
Ability to deal with change	✔	✔	✔		✔	✔		
Willingness to take risks	✔	✔	✔		✔	✔		
Knowing the big picture			✔	✔	✔		✔	✔

Table 4.1   *The learning methods compared*

becomes a learning community within which all managers can gain the most from each other and contribute the most. The sets can provide an opportunity for personal reflection on what has been done, and to provide useful insights and reflections into each manager's behaviour.

Action learning can be organized in several ways. One way is to exchange managers between different organizations. This ensures that managers work on problems with which they are unfamiliar. Another is for managers to be seconded to other departments in their own organization, on work outside their own personal experience. A third method is for managers to stay in their own organizations and their own departments, and work on a particular novel problem, perhaps on a part-time basis. There have also been attempts to link action learning with formal management training programmes. This, however, goes against the ideas of the greatest advocate of action learning, Professor Reg Revans. Clearly, action learning is one of the best ways to achieve learning on the job.

Coaching and counselling

This is the process by which a manager systematically discusses a particular problem in order that he or she may solve it more effectively. The discussion takes place with a colleague or with the manager's boss. Every manager should be able to both give and benefit from coaching and counselling in this way. It is certainly not intended that the boss or colleague actually solves the problem for the manager. The purpose is for the counsellor to act as a 'sounding board' for the manager, helping him to think more clearly about his experiences and learn more, either about himself or about the problem.

Coaching and counselling both involve much more than simple informal discussion, and an effective counsellor needs a range of skills. Counselling has, of course, been extended to many other activities, for example marriage guidance, where it is suited to the kind of personal problems requiring deeper insight into one's own behaviour and motivations. At its best, it can result in the enhancement of self-awareness, changes in behaviour and the development of a range of skills.

Resource centre learning

This is one of the most straightforward approaches to training and development, in which the learner has access to a range of learning resources and a choice about what, when, and how he or she will use them. The resources will typically include books, articles, audio-visual material, and increasingly computer-based learning materials and a range of databases providing information on a worldwide basis.

This approach puts the responsibility fairly and squarely on the learners, and assumes that they have the necessary skills to exercise that responsibility. The trainer, therefore, must see that the learner has the necessary range of skills to capitalize fully on the resource centre. Those skills usually have to be acquired before the resource centre is introduced, or the approach will not be fully effective. The approach must be discussed and agreed with the learner and specific aims set. The advantages of the approach are flexibility, since the learner can attend the centre whenever convenient. Suitable resources can be acquired and changed over time. The approach is best suited for knowledge acquisition over a wide range of subjects.

Business simulations

Business simulations provide an environment within which individuals communicate with one another, argue, negotiate, compromise and eventually come to conclusions. Participants have to deal with information—some quantitative, some qualitative—set objectives, meeting some of them while failing to meet others. They experience the results of their own actions and have to deal with the many uncertainties introduced by their own incomplete understanding of the situation, and by a host of possible outside agencies, including the actions of competitors. Simulations obviously cannot offer real experience, but they do offer the next best thing, vicarious experience, in which most participants become fully involved.

Provided sufficient time is allowed between decision times to reflect on the results achieved and plan for the future, the simulation allows participants to move continually around the four phases of the Kolb experiential learning model, as shown in Figure 4.3. The repetitive nature of the simulation is particularly powerful in this respect.

Although a business simulation starts from a pre-arranged scenario, participants diverge more and more from this as they make successive decisions. Provided that the major influence on their results is their own actions, rather than random factors or the actions of competitors which they are powerless to control, then they will obviously have created their own experience. Under these circumstances participants cannot blame anyone else for their results, and they will truly 'own' their own results.

Simulations offer a number of advantages, including risk-free experimentation, and given a suitably-designed simulation, the ability to study a wide range of situations. Business simulations are more dynamic than almost any other kind of learning method. They can generate unforeseen sets of circumstances, and therefore can provide powerful learning opportunities. Learners are intellectually, emotionally and often physically involved throughout the simulation.

Simulations are good at providing insights into the totality of systems, particularly complex business or economic ones. The learner can therefore be encouraged to adopt a more 'global' view, leading to improved understanding of the organization as a whole, and of constituent parts in their overall context. There is also the opportunity for specific skill development, for example teamworking, decision making, or analytical skills, or in the use of decision aids. There is also the need to use time wisely and sift through information, some of which may be of greater importance than others. Face-to-face communications or negotiations can also be an important feature.

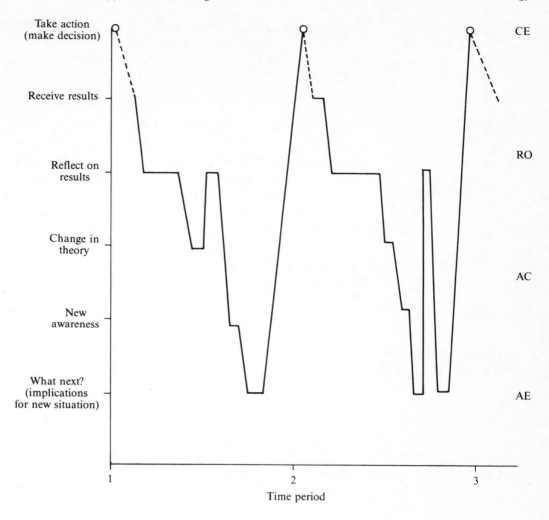

Figure 4.3 *Learning through a simulation*

Simulations also have a number of disadvantages. Tailor-made simulations can be extremely time-consuming to design and they need great preparation and care to run, both by the game administrator and the participants. Simulations can be seen as remote and impersonal if too much stress is placed on the computer as a central feature, rather than as merely an aid to the production of results.

If the purpose of the exercise is purely the improvement of communication skills or to study behavioural issues, there are simpler methods which can be used. Simulations need to be based on a researched (or assumed) model of the situation being simulated. This is the reason why design can be such a lengthy process. Simulations can place great demands on the administrator, who has to fulfil a variety of roles, including that of an adviser, facilitator and analyst. Chapters 5 to 7 deal with these issues in detail.

If the simulation is too simple, participants try and 'beat the game'. If it is too complex the tendency may be to give up the analysis and start guessing. Players may also become so obsessed with winning at all costs that they adopt an aggressive win/lose approach, or overlook some obvious but less attractive alternative. The very level of motivation and involvement engendered by most simulations can itself bring dangers if the participants become distracted from the particular issues which the game administrator wishes to focus on.

There is possibly one danger of using a simulation in a real organization. New strategies or new insights into working relationships could emerge which could threaten the status quo. These, of course, could be exactly what is required—a fundamental reappraisal of 'how things might be'—but the result might be not what was required or anticipated.

Simulations should, therefore, compare well with other learning methods, for the reasons that they comply experiential learning theory, they are clearly motivational, performance-oriented and allow for the observation of a wide range of behaviours over compressed timescales.

Outdoor management development

A relatively recent method in management training, outdoor management development (OMD) activities, gives participants the experience of problem solving, leadership, followership and teamworking roles when working in groups on a range of practical tasks. The approach has much in common with methods used in the training of military officers. Such is the popularity of these methods that there are now some 140 organizations supplying OMD in the UK alone.

Typical activities involve building a bridge, canoeing, rock climbing, potholing, camping and navigational and other less physical exercises. The outdoor events are usually run in an intensive manner which totally preoccupies participants, and therefore such activities can lead to a high level of physical stress and tiredness. It is important that the tasks are chosen carefully with the particular group of participants clearly in mind.

This approach to management development clearly focuses on the leadership and man-management part of a manager's job. However, these methods require those conducting the exercise to have several different kinds of expertise including:

- The ability to give a conceptual view of, say leadership skills and styles, in order to provide a framework for what participants will experience during the exercise.
- Technical skills in whatever activity is being undertaken, e.g. rock climbing or bridge building. The organizers need to know not only the best way to conduct these activities safely, and provide the necessary equipment, but they must also have the ability to teach basic skills to others in a way that will give confidence.
- Observational and behavioural skills to ensure that each participant's

part in the exercise is observed and analysed, and the implications are pointed out. A great deal of tension can arise during outdoor activities and it is vital for there to be a thorough debriefing session during or after the activity. On a practical note it can be very useful to make a video recording of the outdoor events for the purpose of reminding participants what was actually said or done in the 'heat of the moment', and what the effects were, thus facilitating the reflection process once the event is over.

There are a number of advantages of outdoor methods. Because of their intensity, they can give insights into participants' strengths and weaknesses that are not available in other ways. Personal confidence can be increased and hitherto unknown inner resources can be discovered. The management processes of motivation, communication and leadership are made crystal clear and experiences and insights gained during such an exercise are vivid and enduring.

However, not everyone relishes the physical exercise aspects of outdoor training, and those with a disability or in poor health may find it hard to take part unless their individual abilities are taken care of sensitively. Also the physical exercise elements of OMD may not be as acceptable in some cultures.

Case studies The case approach to management development can be traced back over 100 years to the Harvard Law School, when selections from court decisions were used as the basis for class discussion. It took about 50 years for the same methods to be applied in business education in the USA. Cases were introduced to rectify some of the deficiencies of lectures, providing active participation and practical illustrations of material discussed in the lectures. Although the USA has remained the main proponent of the case method, the approach has spread widely. A number of specialist journals have appeared dealing with case studies and the case method has become so popular that there are now over 20 case clearing houses around the world.

Cases describe the subject matter in a practical setting. They usually consist of a problem that a particular real-life organization has faced, and either a description of what action was taken, or the invitation for the learner to devise a suitable course of action for himself or herself. The participant is now no longer a listener, but can contribute ideas and debate with others the merits of what was done, or of his or her own proposals. Advocates of the case approach cite a number of major advantages compared with lectures:

1 Cases can be used to illustrate complex or theoretical concepts. The case must therefore be carefully chosen, bearing in mind the current knowledge of participants, and the particular stage of training they are undergoing.
2 Cases expose students to real-life problems. This is most appropriate in executive training where managers bring their own experience to

bear on a subject, and less appropriate in junior or undergraduate programmes.
3 Cases improve the ability to absorb written information, analyse the situation described and develop solutions (the 'mental agility' competence).
4 Cases develop the ability to explain and defend proposed courses of action verbally and orally, since there is often the need to debate the case in groups before making a presentation to the rest of the class (the 'social and communication' competence).

However, there is continuing debate about the lack of evidence (as opposed to conjecture), showing that case studies work better than other methods. Cases also have a number of drawbacks:

1 They do not really involve participants. They refer to other people in a different organization, in different circumstances, at a different moment in time.
2 Although there are many ways that cases can be run, critics have observed that many trainers still tend to dominate proceedings. Cases certainly do not diminish the role of trainers compared with their role as lecturers, but put different demands upon them.
3 Cases focus on past events, the results of which are usually known. There is no sense of the dynamic unfolding of events, of not knowing what happens next, that is characteristic of some other learning methods.
4 They offer no scope for participants to alter the course of events, and the effects of different actions they propose can only be conjectured.
5 Run properly, they require a great deal of preparation by the trainer.
6 They need not necessarily encourage users to make appropriate generalizations, unless guidance is provided by the trainer.
7 When studied in groups, cases can allow some students to opt out and take little part in the proceedings. However, self-respect and fear of being 'caught out' usually minimizes this danger.

For a detailed discussion of the merits and drawbacks of case studies, see Argyris (1980) and Osigweh (1989).

Lectures   Good lectures are undoubtedly one of the most efficient ways of imparting the maximum amount of factual information to a large number of people in a given time. However, it is useless giving information unless it is clearly understood by listeners and is combined with existing knowledge in the best way to provide new understanding. In some cases lectures offer little opportunity for feedback from learners to the lecturer, although a sensitive lecturer will provide adequate opportunity for this to happen and will therefore be able to judge how the material is being received. Lectures are probably least appropriate for mature action-oriented people. For that reason many management courses have moved away from lecture-based methods.

In a mixed audience, lectures have to be pitched at the average level of knowledge of the audience and so offer little opportunity for tailoring to the needs of the individual. While useful for imparting information or analytical arguments, lectures are clearly not effective in developing skills since they offer no opportunity for practice. The most powerful limitation of the lecture is the lack of active involvement of the learner, and indeed not all listeners have the ability to give their full attention for a sufficient length of time. This is the main reason why studies show that much information imparted in a lecture is quickly forgotten. A powerful speaker can nevertheless give an audience an enthusiasm for a subject, which will act as a spur for further learning.

Since lectures are largely one-way communications, managers used to an active style of work find it hard to adapt to the largely passive listening role required unless a great deal of audience participation is provided. More active learning methods, allowing people to make immediate use of new information, are more likely to be acceptable.

How do the learning methods compare in practice?

There have been several attempts to compare the value of lectures, case studies and simulations on an objective basis. However, the range of simulations, cases, lecturers, and educational settings is so diverse and the measurement problems so great that comparison is very difficult.

Early research sought the opinions of people who had experienced both simulations and case studies. Later attempts were made to measure objectively participants' knowledge before and after taking part in such activities. McKenney (1963) found that simulations were more effective than cases in helping people to understand planning concepts. Raia (1966) found that people who had participated in business simulations scored more highly in written examinations than those who had not taken part. Moutinho (1988) reported on several studies showing that simulations produce favourable student attitudes, increased satisfaction and involvement, and increased learning and long-term retention of marketing concepts.

The research also shows another interesting result. Simple simulations, with few decision inputs per period, allow as much or more learning than complex ones with more decision inputs. Also, significant learning only occurs after the simulation rules have been mastered, showing that participants can only learn from a simulation once they have learned about it.

Wolfe prepared a comprehensive review of research into the teaching effectiveness of games and simulations from 1973 to 1983, and found some evidence showing that games and simulations were more effective than other teaching methods, but the evidence was by no means compelling. This was partly due to the immense difficulty of conducting genuine research in a notoriously difficult context, in particular due to the difficulty of measuring knowledge gains using objective methods rather than by self-assessment (Wolfe, 1985).

The research into the effectiveness of gaming, conducted over many years, indicates that simulations are useful methods of learning, and are probably more effective for many purposes than other methods, particularly in complex areas such as business strategy. However, the best results are achieved when simulations are used in conjunction with other learning methods. Figure 4.2 supports this, by showing that no one learning method is able to provide all the knowledge and skills required by managers.

References

Argyris, C., 1980 'Some Limitations of the Case Method: Exercises in a Management Development Program' in *Academy of Management Review*, vol. 8, no. 2, pp. 329–33.

Bateson, G., 1973 *Steps to an Ecology of Mind*, Ballantine Books, NY.

Garratt, R., 1987 *The Learning Organisation*, Fontana/Collins.

Honey, P. and Mumford, A., 1992 *The Manual of Learning Styles*, Honey, Maidenhead.

Honey, P. and Mumford, A., 1986 *Using your learning style*, Honey, Maidenhead.

Kelly, G. A., 1955 *The Psychology of Personal Constructs*, New York, Norton.

Kolb, D. A., Rubin, I. M. and Osland, J. M., 1991 *Organisational Behaviour: An Experiential Approach*, 5th edition, Prentice Hall, Englewood Cliffs, N J.

Kolb, D. A., Spring 1976 'Management and the Learning Process' in *California Management Review*, vol. XVIII, no. 3, pp. 21–31.

McKenney, J. L., 1963 'Evaluation of Decision Simulation as a Learning Environment' in *Management Technology*, vol. 3, no. 1, pp. 56–67.

Moutinho, L., Winter 1988 'Learning/Teaching Effectiveness of Marketing Simulation Games' in *The Quarterly Review of Marketing*, pp. 10–14.

Osigweh, C. A. B., 1989 'Casing the Case Approach in Management Development' in *Journal of Management Development*, vol. 8, no. 2, pp. 41–57.

Pedler, M., Burgoyne, J. and Boydell, T., 1986 *A Manager's Guide to Self-Development*, McGraw-Hill.

Raia, P. A., 1966 'A Study of the Educational Value of Management Games' in *Journal of Business*, vol. 39, pp. 339–52.

Woodruffe, C., September 1991 'Competent by Any Other Name' in *Personnel Management*, pp. 30–33.

Wolfe, J., 1985 'The Teaching Effectiveness of Games in Collegiate Business Courses' in *Simulation and Games*, vol. 16, no. 3, pp. 251–88.

5 The design process

This chapter will give readers an indication of what is involved in simulation design, from the designer's and the client's points of view. We are mainly concerned with the design of model-based simulations, although many of the issues discussed apply to most types of simulation. Designing business simulations can require a great deal of time and effort and involve a combination of creative, practical, consulting and project management skills. However, apart from the usefulness of the final product the design process can be a highly rewarding one, offering insights and learning opportunities for all concerned.

Before discussing the design process itself, there are a few essential preliminary issues which must be handled properly if the design work is to succeed. The first and most obvious question is whether it is necessary to design a new simulation at all. Are there any existing suitable simulations, or ones which could be modified for the desired purpose? Therefore we start by discussing how to decide whether to use an existing simulation or to design a new one.

Given that no suitable ready-made simulation exists, there may be no alternative but to design one. This process is much easier with a simulation built around a hypothetical organization or situation. In this case we can design our own simulation and no one can argue that the issues and relationships contained in it are incorrect. The process becomes more difficult, but in many ways more worth while, when a simulation is to be tailor-made for a particular organization. In this case the designer has to develop a model of the organization, as seen through the eyes of the clients, which is realistic and detailed enough to allow the construction of the simulation, and yet which is not unnecessarily complex, and above all which meets clear learning objectives. This chapter describes methods to assist in this process.

Due to the scale of the work involved in designing a new tailor-made simulation, it is usually essential to form a design team, drawing people from a variety of backgrounds from within the organization concerned, to share the work and to ensure that wide experience is available. The various roles involved in this team are discussed, as well as the need to manage the whole process carefully.

The simulation design process is a particularly fascinating one. The act of bringing to life ideas held on paper or in people's minds about what the simulation should contain and about how it might work is a rewarding experience, almost like creating a living thing. It is certainly a process that is best experienced first-hand and readers wishing to learn about this process themselves would be well advised to work with an experienced designer and 'learn by doing'. This chapter will provide a good start.

Off-the-shelf or tailor-made?

Deciding whether to design a new simulation or use an existing one depends critically on the purpose we have in mind. It is therefore essential to be clear about our precise learning objectives before investigating simulations already on the market. There are many possible learning objectives, including practising or improving some group of managerial skills, demonstrating an area of the business to those unfamiliar with it, for teambuilding purposes, or encouraging change by putting people through unfamiliar tasks or new approaches to familiar ones. Chapter 8 contains a number of case studies illustrating these possible uses in detail.

There are a number of reference books and periodicals which describe some of the simulations available, but unfortunately information on the more complex computer-based simulations that are now available is very hard to come by. The reading list at the end of this book contains further information, and the journals mentioned there will provide a series of more theoretically based articles. Appendix 2 contains a list of suppliers and describes a representative set of simulations they have produced. This will give readers an idea of the wide variety of computer-based simulations available in the UK and elsewhere.

The following set of questions will be useful in helping readers to decide whether an existing simulation is appropriate.

Participants

1 How many and what type of decisions or issues are included in the simulation?
2 Does the simulation involve problem-solving or decision-making issues relevant to our participants?
3 How long will it take for participants to become familiar with the exercise? Is this appropriate for us?
4 Are there natural roles and responsibilities for participants to assume? Are these suitable for our purpose?
5 Does the simulation provide appropriate interaction between teams, and between participants in the same team?
6 How many participants can take part per management team? How many in total? Are all participants likely to be fully involved?

The organization

1 What types of issues and experiences does the simulation represent? Are these appropriate?
2 Are the special features of our organization, i.e. products and services, processes, reporting systems, type and volume of information, adequately represented in the simulation?

3 What degree of 'in-house' jargon do we need? Will users reject a simulation couched in general business language? Is it part of the purpose to encourage participants to get used to a particular new set of terminology or reporting procedures?

4 What is the timescale represented by the simulation? Do we wish to deal with day-to-day issues, or to encourage a long-term perspective?

Industrial setting

1 How strongly competitive is our industry, and is this reflected in the simulation?

2 What are the economic, market or competitive conditions represented by the simulation? Are the markets 'zero sum'? For example, if a team does something to stimulate one additional order, has this order been 'stolen' from a competitor, or is it from a new customer who did not exist previously?

3 Is the simulation up-to-date in ways that matter, i.e. pay rates, tax rates, inflation rates? Can it be easily modified as time progresses to capture important changes? What will be the cost of this?

Results

1 Does the simulation provide for adequate feedback of results, and are these sufficiently clearly related to decisions made or actions taken by participants?

2 Are the rewards and penalties for relatively good and poor performance clear?

3 What kind and volume of results are produced—how valid are these? Are graphs provided?

4 How will 'winners and losers' be decided (if necessary)?

5 What special operating and reporting practices do we wish to include? It is sometimes useful to design the simulation to provide results in a particular fashion, perhaps to represent the current type of management reports in use in the organization, or to allow people to adjust to new ones.

External events

1 Are there chance elements? Do we wish to include either a novel feature such as a strike, a factory burned down, or a new market opportunity suddenly arising?

2 To what extent are the results of team decisions immune from random or chance influences? If the decisions were repeated under identical circumstances, would the same results be achieved? Is some degree of uncertainty involved?

Using the simulation

1 Is the simulation fully computer-operated? What manual calculations need to be done? What analysis or calculations do we want our participants to do, if any?

2 Are the instructions to participants and administrators clear and comprehensive?

3 Is the documentation complete and well presented? Can we obtain sufficient copies?

4 How much do administrators need to know about computers to run the simulation?

5 Do we have someone who can operate the simulation, explain it to our intended participants, and act as impartial umpire where necessary?

6 If it is necessary to involve an outsider, how experienced and acceptable will he or she be to our participants?

7 Has the simulation been fully tested? Can we contact some existing users to find out their opinions?

8 How often will we use it? Does it represent value for money?

9 Is it usable on our computer equipment?

10 Can we examine a copy of the simulation and documentation before buying, and preferably try it out first?

11 If appropriate, is the simulation accompanied by suitable decision support software, i.e. spreadsheets for use on a 'what if?' basis? Can such software be easily developed?

12 Is the simulation complex enough to prevent rejection by participants, yet not so complex that it defies analysis?

Designing a tailor-made simulation

Having decided that it is worth while designing a tailor-made simulation, a few words of warning are essential. The design process can be a long one, but given commitment of designer and client, it can often provide not only a highly satisfactory result, but can be an illuminating process in itself.

Practical considerations dictate that if the time available is limited then this will severely limit what can be achieved. The best advice that can be given here is that design nearly always takes longer than you think. The author has never yet overestimated the time it will take to design a simulation. Simulation design is in many ways a voyage of discovery and, like explorers, we never know what hazards have to be faced on the journey, so we can therefore never accurately predict how long it will take to achieve our goals. Figure 5.1 shows a highly simplified schematic diagram of some of the issues which have to be covered during the design process.

The discovery of the most important issues to be included in the simulation, and the relationships between them, is itself a learning experience for the designers. This is because the very act of designing a simulation based on a particular part of the organization forces those concerned to answer a series of penetrating questions about how the business works, what the really important issues are, and how these interrelate. We sometimes have to answer questions which have not been asked before, and perhaps which have not even been imagined. For example: 'What would happen if a range of different economic circumstances prevailed?' or 'How would customers react if we invested heavily in after-sales service?'

Before the designer can develop the model on which the simulation is based, he or she must have a clear idea of what the crucial business issues are. This is not to say that he or she need discover the exact 'reality' of the relationships that underlie the real world problem the simulation

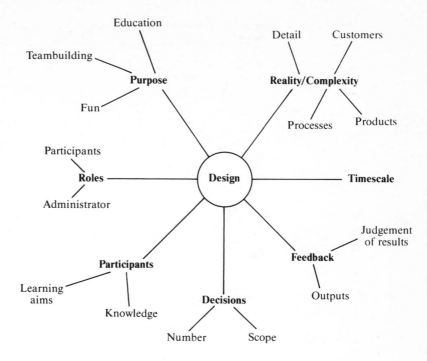

Figure 5.1 *Design issues*

is based upon, but the model must not be counter-intuitive and must not include relationships which are clearly different from reality. It is therefore necessary to understand how the business works, sometimes in a fair degree of detail before designing the simulation.

It may be helpful to remember that the type of simulation dealt with here is the model-based simulation which accepts inputs (decisions made by participants, inputs from the environment, other participants or the simulation administrator) and produces a range of outputs, including operational and financial results. The simulation will incorporate a set of cause-effect relationships which are sufficiently realistic to allow appropriate outputs to be generated from any conceivable input, and yet not be so complex as to prevent players learning enough to act in sensible ways as they take part in the simulation.

The model is computer-based for speed and accuracy, and its purpose is to show the effects of various input or decision variables on output variables. The purpose of the simulation is to show the consequences of various plans or strategies, and to demonstrate to participants the results of these actions. Models are always selective and simplified representations of reality, and since the model is designed and constructed by an individual or a group of individuals, there must be consensus on design (Hammond, 1974). The techniques described below encourage group involvement and consensus formation. The design process will be described under the nine headings shown in Table 5.1.

Table 5.1 *The simulation design process*

---

1 *Working methods*
   Roles in simulation design
   Managing the project

2 *Purpose*
   Participants
   Learning objectives
   Roles
   Administrator
   Context

3 *Concept*
   Decisions
   Timescale
   Outputs
   External events
   Complexity
   Predictability
   Customer influences
   Interaction
   Other issues

4 *Qualitative model*
   Techniques for discovering model relationships
   Mapping relationships

5 *Quantitative model*
   Cause-effect tables
   Finding the 'shape' of relationships
   Operational and financial aspects

6 *Programming the simulation*
   Prototyping
   Data collection

7 *Testing and validation*
   Credibility
   Preparing the simulation for others to run

8 *Documentation*
   For administrators
   For participants

9 *Developing the simulation*

Table 5.1 shows the design steps in a somewhat idealized sequence. In reality the process does not usually happen in this logical order. Sometimes we do not start from a clearly stated objective; we begin where it is easiest, perhaps by establishing the major decisions which will be made by the participants, the type of situation we wish the simulation to include, or perhaps the type and detail of results that must be produced. Figure 5.2 shows what often happens in practice.

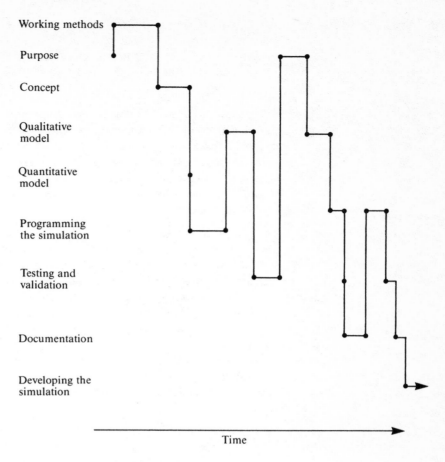

Working methods

Purpose

Concept

Qualitative
model

Quantitative
model

Programming
the simulation

Testing and
validation

Documentation

Developing the
simulation

Time

Figure 5.2 *The actual design process*

Wherever we start, the steps in design seldom proceed in a sequential linear fashion. Very often several different stages are carried out at the same time and loops and repetitions occur. Under these circumstances the 'prototyping' method of program design is most appropriate. Using this approach a simplified version of the simulation is produced quickly, demonstrated to the client, and continually revised. During the process the design team progressively refines its ideas on the purpose and design of the simulation. This method will be used in what follows.

Chapter 6 illustrates the first few stages of the design process using a simple example based on a hypothetical company. All readers are recommended to read Chapter 6 and the further details contained in Appendix I if they wish to gain a fuller understanding of the design process as a whole.

So, with the warnings expressed above about the difficulties and rewards in designing a tailor-made simulation, let us proceed to the first stage shown in Table 5.1. The first need is to establish clearly how the designer, client and others involved in the design will carry out the work.

1 Working methods

A tailor-made simulation will seldom be designed by one individual. Usually a team will be involved including the designer and a number of managers and trainers from the client organization. There are a number of roles which must be performed in this process.

Roles in simulation design

The designer needs to have the ability to work with the client to clarify the objectives of the simulation and the issues it should contain. Some of the methods used in this process are described below. The designer should also advise on what is practicable and what is not, since there is a natural tendency to make things too complex, and clients sometimes have to be persuaded to simplify things. This role requires consultancy skills of a high order.

The next role needed by the designer is that of modeller, helping to decide how the variables and interrelationships discussed can be used to build the required model. Closely allied with this is the role of programmer, translating the agreed design into an appropriate programming language. This part of the process will usually be hidden from the client's view, but the client will need to be constantly kept in touch with what is going on, using the prototyping approach. The designer must adopt an appropriate professional approach which is much closer to that of a business consultant than that of a programmer. Indeed, the computer is best left alone until confidence and rapport are established between client and designer, and the first qualitative stages of design are complete.

The client has a number of roles too. Firstly, as sponsor of the work he or she will ultimately be responsible for what is done and when. This will obviously involve agreeing the overall scope and purpose of the simulation. It is often essential to have a project champion, sometimes the individual whose idea it was to design the simulation. The champion is ideally in an influential position to promote the design activity within the organization and to secure the necessary resources to carry out the work.

The client is the content expert, knowing about the business and its setting, the competitive and economic factors, typical behaviour of companies in the sector, and what he or she hopes the simulation will achieve. The client will also be responsible for selecting the design team, including people who can provide specialist expertise or provide the required information, for example to advise on how any financial statements should be laid out and provide the necessary financial data.

Managing the project

Finally, there is the client's most important duty, to manage the project and to agree the working methods to be used. The client will need to ensure that the right people, from outside the core design team, are called upon at the appropriate time, and that sufficient publicity is given to the simulation during the design and after completion. It is also the client's responsibility, working with the designer, to set the agenda for the design meetings and agree a timescale with major milestones.

Regular meetings must be held throughout all stages of the design to agree design parameters, gather necessary information, demonstrate progress and to discuss any difficulties arising. The prototyping approach will usually mean that the designer regularly demonstrates the simulation as it develops. This work must be treated like any other major project, including the agreements of various stages of design, and recording of the overall scope, objectives and setting of the simulation. Particular attention must be paid to who else in the client organization needs to know about the design project, or whose support may be necessary, particularly if they are not part of the core design team. Having laid the groundwork the next stage of design is to agree the detailed objectives of the simulation and for whom it is intended.

It is not sufficient for the simulation to be well designed. For the simulation to be successful it is also essential that the client and design team are fully involved at all times in the design process. To leave the user out of the design process at any stage is a sure recipe for disaster. If trust and understanding are built up at an early stage it is much more likely that the simulation will be designed and used successfully. This will occur much more naturally if people have really been involved in design. The key to success is continued communication between client, designer and design team.

2 Purpose

The purpose, context, scope and limitations of the simulation should be clearly agreed. This is the most important stage of design and often the most difficult one, since unwise design decisions made now may be hard to amend at a later stage. It is often as much of a problem deciding what to leave out as what to include.

Participants

Whatever the purpose, the designer has to produce a simulation that will not only meet that purpose for the intended participants, but do so in a way that captures their interest. So we must consider the intended participants very carefully. What are their aims and objectives? What are their attitudes to the simulation likely to be? What is their previous experience or knowledge of such exercises? What is their level of business knowledge, responsibilities and intellectual abilities? How well-equipped are they to deal with subjects not immediately within their own experience? How well can they operate as a team? These are typical of the type of questions that must be resolved. In practice, the client, very often the training manager, will have resolved the questions in his or her mind, but they will have to be clearly understood by the design team as a whole.

When the time comes to run the simulation, thought must also be given to the formality of the organization in which the participants are employees. Is it bureaucratic and status-conscious? Is it flexible and can people move around across boundaries as the needs of the job require? How homogeneous will the group of participants be? Will there be any boss-subordinate relationships, and if so are participants likely to get

fully involved in the simulation if they know that their boss or other
superior colleague are present?

Learning objectives   The design team should agree at an early stage what the key learning
objectives of the simulation are, and express these as simply as possible.
For example, a simulation developed some years ago was designed for
junior managers from a particular organization, and the main objective
was:

'to give participants an insight into how the activities of their department affect
other departments, and how different areas of the business interact to produce
overall business and financial performance.'

Participants in the simulation were fairly junior managers who generally
only had experience of one function of the company, and would therefore only know well colleagues from within their own function. The
simulation provided the opportunity to work with managers from other
departments and functions, and gave an overall view of the business.
Not much time was available so the simulation had to be easy to understand and quick to run. These considerations led to a simulation in
which the same set of decisions were repeated each simulated time
period. One page of results was produced for each team and many simplifications were made in the company operating procedures and
reports (i.e. staff, once hired, were fully productive immediately, and
staff did not voluntarily leave the company).

Note that in this example the participants and their specific educational
needs came first. The simulation was deliberately simplified, and did not
represent each department of the business it portrayed in anything like
realistic terms. It focused on demonstrating the need for managers in
different parts of the business to understand the business as a whole,
and to show the interrelationships between decisions taken in each
department. It produced results which would demonstrate these issues
in factual and financial terms.

Participant roles   Whether participants assume particular roles or not will depend on the
purpose of the simulation. Roles add a dimension of reality, and in a
complex simulation they may be essential. However, too rigid allocation
of roles can mean that participants only gain an understanding of one
aspect of the simulation, in the same way that managers in a real business can often only gain experience of their own department. The roles
can also lead to interpersonal conflict, although this too is realistic and
may be part of the purpose of the simulation.

The administrator   However elegant and useful the simulation might be, it must be simple
enough to administer, or it will not be used. Issues to be resolved here
include the extent to which the administrators will be expected to intervene in the running of the simulation, whether any subjective judge-
ments will be required, or whether results will depend purely on the
decisions made by participants. The administrator's level of computer

expertise will also influence the design. Some degree of training will be essential if the simulation is to be run by anyone other than the designers.

Context One issue here is whether the simulation takes place in one place at one time, or is interspersed with other activities, perhaps spread over several days as part of a course, or run remotely by post. In addition it is important to decide whether it will be possible to brief participants personally before the simulation starts, or whether this must be done in writing. All these questions will have implications for the complexity, type and amount of briefing, documentation and design of the simulation.

3 Concept

The conceptual stage of simulation design now takes place. The purpose is to agree the overall scope of the simulation and ensure it meets the users' needs. Agreement must be reached on the major issues to be included in the model and how these are related to one another. A question that must be addressed at an early stage is how much detail should be included in the simulation itself. For example, simulations representing a large part of an organization's operations will usually be expressed in much less detail than those dealing solely with marketing or production issues. The temptation to believe that 'the more complex the better' must be avoided.

The crucial test is that the simulation must have an acceptable degree of realism and credibility. For example, in most markets if the price of a product or service increases then sales volumes will fall. Also for the sake of morale among participants, the simulation should not allow one team to dominate a market too easily. The following are among the main issues which need to be agreed at this stage.

Decisions What decisions will participants have to make? The aim here is that all decision areas should have approximately the same level of importance, and that collectively they should cover the design purpose of the simulation. Will these be repeated every time period? How quickly will the results of those decisions become apparent within the simulation?

Timescale What are appropriate time intervals? Will these be the same throughout the simulation? The question of timescale should be appropriate to the overall purpose of the simulation, and will be related to the strategic level of the decisions involved.

Outputs How much and what type of information will be available? Examples are market share, cost, income, profitability, and product or service quality or quantity. The required type and detail of financial reports must also be agreed. Other questions include whether or not the same information is to be provided throughout the simulation, and whether it is to be produced free of charge.

External events What external events, outside the control of participants, will be included? These could include economic factors such as inflation, currency movements, and trade cycles or natural disasters.

Complexity   The degree of complexity and reality required will follow from the overall simulation objectives, keeping in mind the type of participant. What is an appropriate number and type of products and markets? What are the means of promotion, advertising and distribution? What degree of personnel detail is required, for example hiring, payment or motivation of staff? What degrees of detail on production processes, materials and stocks are required?

The issue can usually be resolved by reference to the overall purpose of the exercise and by the need to keep the simulation as simple as possible consistent with that purpose. If the simulation is directed at marketing executives their concerns might be, for example, how best to promote or distribute goods in a particular market, and it might therefore be sufficient to group goods together into broad categories. On the other hand, if the simulation is aimed at retailers, then other issues such as pricing or display would be equally important and products might be grouped into different categories for that purpose. Different sets of decisions are then required according to the two different uses.

Predictability   What chance events will there be? How much will these be hinted at in the documentation? The designers must be especially careful here not to introduce too much randomness. Random events might well be a useful way of representing the unpredictable events occurring in reality, and they are easy to reproduce in a computer program, but too much randomness can make the simulation difficult for participants. The crucial factor is that the major long-run influences on results must be the decisions that participants themselves make, or those of competitors. If progress is largely outside their hands then a sense of helplessness will quickly ensue.

Customer influences   What customers are to be included in the simulation? What are the major influences on customers within each market? How important are they? How much must simulation-produced results mirror reality? These questions are discussed in some detail under Sections 4 and 5 below.

Interaction   What is an appropriate degree of interaction between participants and between teams? Must all teams remain separate, or will any formal relationships or alliances be allowed between them? What informal relationships or agreements are to be encouraged or forbidden? How much of a team's results will depend on their own decisions and how much on those of their competitors, and on factors outside their control?

As outlined in Chapter 3, there are several types of interaction, among them being personal interaction and model interaction. Personal interaction occurs naturally all the time and in many ways, particularly when a group of managers sit down together to tackle a problem. This type of interaction will happen whether or not participants adopt roles.

Model interaction means the degree of impact that one team's decisions has on the results generated by other teams. This is usually felt most in the market for the goods or services represented in the simulation. For example, if a team does something to gain 100 extra orders for its products, the model interaction can determine how many of those 100 orders are 'stolen' from other competing teams, and how many are genuinely new customers that had not appeared in the simulation before.

Other issues   There may be a variety of other issues to consider, including the following:

1 To what extent are any markets for goods or services fixed in size?
2 How much of the industry supply chain will be included—purchasing, production operations, delivery, after-sales operations?
3 Will participants input decisions themselves, or will decisions be input by the administrator?
4 Will any degree of experimentation be allowed, perhaps using a 'what if?' model?

Having decided the overall purpose and concept of the simulation, we now proceed to the design of the model itself. The model must show exactly how the decisions and other inputs are used to produce results. Because this is the most difficult part of the design process, it is broken down into two stages involving largely qualitative and quantitative processes respectively.

4 Qualitative model

Where the designer has been given a broad educational brief and can design the simulation as he or she wishes, this part of the design process is relatively straightforward. The decision variables and other variables can be chosen by the designer, and the relationships between them created as required. This situation arises where the area of application is so well understood that the situation can be modelled fairly easily, or when the details can be invented to suit the purpose.

However, when the simulation is tailor-made for a particular client, the design problems can be more severe. The simulation must take account of the special needs of the client and the participants. Above all, the simulation must be credible and reflect the clients' views of the relevant managerial and business issues, even when those views may initially be far from clear to the client himself. Nevertheless, there are some parts of the design process that are inherently easier than others. Financial relationships are among the easiest to represent, since they usually have a straightforward logical basis. For example, sales revenue can be calculated by the simple multiplication of sales volume and unit price. Next in order of complexity come a wide range of possible logical relationships. For example, in a production simulation with a finite production lead time it is impossible to sell more items within the lead time than there are items in stock at the start of the period.

The most difficult problems in design are in the construction of the 'behavioural' parts of the model. For example, in a marketing simulation, how will consumers react to changes in pricing and advertising? What are the relative effects of price, promotion, product and position in a particular market? Also in a simulation involving human resource issues, how will employees' morale depend on working conditions, or on pay?

The difficulty arises because the clients have not usually thought about the problem before in the detailed way that is necessary for model construction. Even if they have done so, they can never be certain they have the right answers since in the real world it is seldom possible to check their views by doing an experiment.

Therefore the central problem of simulation design is to make the client's views and beliefs, which are often only subconsciously known, explicit and visible. Techniques are needed to help the client develop and refine his view of the issues, and where there are multiple clients, each of whom has a partial understanding of the problem, to allow all clients to share and compare their perceptions. It must be stated that we are not concerned about the absolute 'truth' or otherwise of those perceptions, but simply to express them clearly and explore their consequences.

The client may have to be encouraged to work through a number of different descriptions of the problem, discarding some parts and refining and developing others. Sometimes as the design proceeds and ideas begin to be refined, previous views about what variables to include, and how they interrelate, will be superseded by better insights. This approach can also highlight the need for additional opinions or data. Sometimes the act of model development will itself demonstrate the need to include other issues or parts of the problem which had not previously been considered.

For this reason simulation design can be a rewarding experience in its own right. It can be helpful in bringing major problems and issues to the surface, and exploring the relationships between them, often giving insights which were not previously available. We now summarize some of the more useful techniques for spelling out clients' perceptions of the issues and relationships involved in the simulation.

Techniques for discovering model relationships

The designer must find some way of expressing, either verbally or graphically, the relationships felt to be important, particularly the relationships between the inputs and outputs already decided. This is why it is so important to have a range of expertise in the design team. The team will have the kind of detailed knowledge of the business which is essential to design the simulation. Unless the business is understood it cannot be simulated. Figure 5.3 indicates that the information required to design the model is often 'invisible' since it exists in the heads and experiences of clients. The invisible model must be made visible.

The methods described will attempt to capture the full richness of the

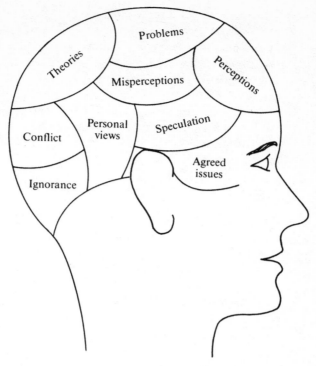

Figure 5.3 *The invisible model*

client's perceptions of that part of the business on which the simulation is based. The methods are similar to the 'soft' consultancy approaches which have been developed to help managers spell out and clarify their problems. These usually involve a combination of group facilitation, creativity and diagrammatic techniques (see Eden, 1979, Moore, 1987). Table 5.2 shows the stages we go through in this process in moving from qualitative to quantitative descriptions of the issues during simulation design.

Table 5.2 *Stages in model design*

• List of issues	Qualitative
—input variables	
—output variables	
—other variables	
• Cause-effect relationships	
• Sign of relationships	
• Strength of relationships	
• Shape of relationships	
• Mathematical relationship	Quantitative

This chapter does not attempt to describe the complete set of techniques which have been developed to explore people's thinking. The interested reader will find more in the list of references at the end of the book. We are concerned with methods that capture these thoughts fully enough for a representation of them to seem adequate to the client and design team, and which are sufficiently detailed to allow logical and mathematical relationships to be developed by the simulation designer. Whatever method is used the results must be easily understood by the client and allow the client's perceptions to arise naturally from discussion. Figure 5.4 shows an example of what we are trying to achieve—a visible model which the designer and the design team can all agree on. This shows in simple terms how two formulae (a) and (b) could be applied to determine a firm's market share, depending on the relative price of a particular product.

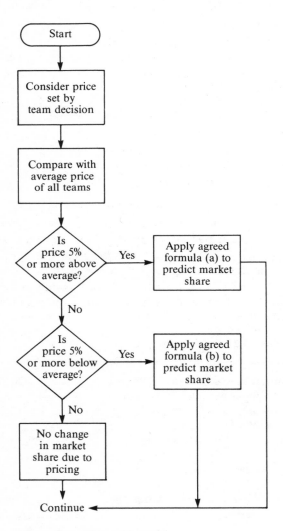

Figure 5.4 *The visible model*

It is important to state that we are not trying to subject people's perceptions of their part of the business to scientific scrutiny. The design team's ideas must be allowed to emerge naturally and the techniques do not seek to rationalize or regulate people's views, even less to decide what is a 'right' or 'wrong' view of an issue.

The knowledge level of the client will usually determine the type of approach used. A sophisticated client might be able to talk in system dynamic terms (see below), perhaps using some purpose-built software to draw out their perceptions. In other cases the designer will have to tread more warily, using some of the simpler approaches. The problem of eliciting information from the client for the design of a business simulation is similar to that facing a knowledge engineer when developing an expert system. Knowledge engineering is difficult because human knowledge is messy and complex. This is because the knowledge has been gained over a long period of time, from many sources, and it is constantly changing. People who have become experts in any activity find it difficult to articulate their knowledge to others less knowledgeable than themselves. For example, an expert geologist's knowledge is often so extensive that it is difficult for him or her to explain it, and this process can take a long time. Generally, the more expert someone is in a particular subject area, the more 'unconscious' their knowledge is and the more difficult it is to explain it to others.

Mapping relationships A number of techniques are available to overcome this problem. They help to identify and map out the relationships among a list of concepts relevant to the simulation. 'Influence diagrams' allow the display of a set of relationships between large numbers of concepts. An influence diagram is a diagrammatic way of capturing someone's beliefs about a particular problem. Its usefulness is that it can display those beliefs about cause-effect relationships graphically, and show the consequences of those beliefs.

The first step is to agree on a set of variables to be used in the simulation. These follow from the decisions, external events and outputs agreed. Then follows the construction of a diagram showing how the variables are connected together. The diagram has the advantage that it is a clear and concise vehicle for the whole design team to share their ideas. A very simple example is shown in Figure 5.5, in which variations in price (a) of a product will lead to variations in market share (b). The direction of the arrow shows the direction of the cause-effect relationship, i.e. price will affect market share and not vice versa.

Price
(a)

Market share
(b)

Figure 5.5 *A simple cause-effect relationship*

The discussion takes place in the design team, and a consensus opinion is required. The diagram then needs to be extended so that it shows whether the effects are positive or negative (i.e. whether an increase in price leads to an increase or decrease in market share), and the strength of the relationships between variables (i.e. how big the changes are). As an example, consider again the market share and selling price of a product. We could once more represent the relationship by connecting the two variables price and market share together with an arrow as shown in Figure 5.6. As before, the direction of the arrow indicates the direction of causality. The negative sign indicates that if price is increased, market share will decrease, and vice versa. A positive sign would indicate that if price is increased, market share will also increase, and vice versa.

Price   Market share
  (a)   (b)

Figure 5.6   *The sign of the relationship*

To take a more complex example, suppose that the client believes that the market share of a product is affected by company reputation and product price. Sales volume is calculated from market share and market size, and both price and sales volume affect revenue. We might represent the situation as shown in Figure 5.7.

The arrows and signs have the same meaning as in the two previous figures. Recursive relationships are allowed, i.e. revenue is allowed to affect price, reputation or market share, or if so, only via time delays to

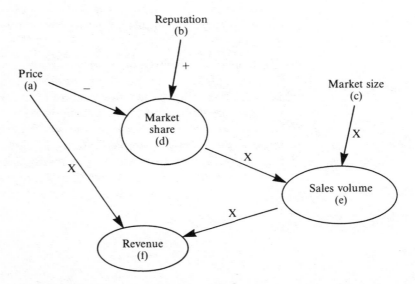

Figure 5.7   *A more realistic influence diagram*

avoid a vicious circle. The Xs' denote a logical or mathematical relationship between the two concepts, for example revenue is derived from the multiplication of price and sales volume.

Drawing influence diagrams is intuitively easy and allows the representation of concepts and the causal relationships which are believed to exist between them. The limitation is that the strengths of these relationships are not shown. The method therefore does not provide sufficient basis on its own for the design of computer-based models and additional steps are necessary.

What we have achieved so far represents an enormous step in simulation design. We have agreed the overall scope and purpose of the simulation, taken into account the needs of both participants and administrators, and decided the overall structure of the simulation and the set of issues to be included. We have also shown qualitatively and diagrammatically how these issues are interrelated. However, whether the simulation is to be manually or computer operated we still have much more to do.

5 Quantitative model

The next stage is the quantitative stage of design. This will specify the relationships between variables, logically and mathematically wherever possible, and represent the internal operations and financial structure of the part of the organization we are simulating. For example, in a marketing simulation we need to establish what the effect would be on a team's market share if the team doubled (or trebled) advertising expenditure, and how quickly that effect would become apparent. Also we need to specify quantitatively what the effects would be on other teams' market shares. We have to replace the qualitative representation developed so far with more specific graphical or logical ones which can be turned into a computer programme.

Cause-effect tables

Cause-effect tables are a method which attempts to show the relative strength of variables. Each part of the influence diagram developed above is taken in turn and a cause-effect table is developed. The influence diagram shown in Figure 5.7 is represented by the cause-effect table shown in Table 5.3. Each causal variable is shown by a row in the table and each effect by a column.

The letters h, m and l are used to indicate whether the effect of a variable is relatively high, medium or low. Table 5.3 shows that company reputation is judged to have a high positive effect on market share, hence the +h, and price has a medium negative effect on market share, hence the −m. The Xs' show a direct logical or financial relationship, for example sales volume is determined by the multiplication of market size and market share, and revenue is determined by the multiplication of price and sales volume. The three levels of high, medium and low strength are useful for the design of mathematical and logical relationships used in the computer program.

Table 5.3 *A cause-effect table*

		Effects		
		Market share (d)	Sales volume (e)	Revenue (f)
Causes	Price (a)	−m		X
	Reputation (b)	+h		
	Market size (c)		X	
	Market share (a)		X	
	Sales volume (e)			X

Finding the 'shape' of relationships

Given the strength of the relationship between two variables, we now need to establish the shape of the relationship. Approaches based upon the ideas of system dynamics (SD) are very useful here. The purpose of SD is to explain systems behaviour and suggest changes in structure or policies that will improve behaviour. In SD an attempt is made to examine each cause/effect relationship over the whole range of possible values (Coyle, 1977). The relationships between variables are not necessarily smooth and regular, as shown in Figure 5.8 which illustrates how the possible output of a product depends upon the demand for it. Excessive demand may in fact cause production difficulties leading in turn to reduced output.

Figure 5.9 shows another example in which a company is making urgent efforts to improve the quality of the service offered to customers.

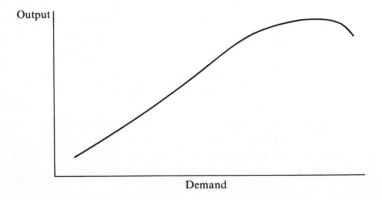

Figure 5.8 The effect of demand on product output

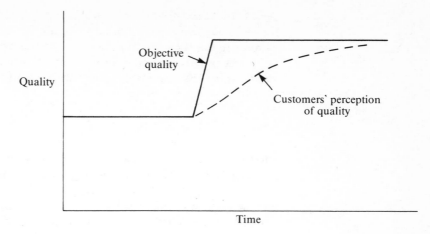

Figure 5.9 *Objective and perceived quality*

Again the relationship between quality and time (or effort) is far from straightforward. Although the company can objectively measure a big improvement in quality over a fairly short timescale, they find that it takes much longer to improve customers' perceptions of quality.

In some cases the design team will know the most appropriate shape for relationships. In other cases it will be the designers' job to help to suggest how to develop sensible relationships that are not counter-intuitive.

The methods used in any particular simulation design are often a combination of those described above. Firstly, the client is invited to describe the overall aims and objectives of the simulation. He is encouraged to speculate freely about the number and type of issues (variables) that are involved. After a suitable period of time a series of influence diagrams are drawn up, usually one for each market or major issue. The maps will be useful to ensure that all relevant issues have been included, and to begin to establish the direction and relative strength of effects.

Following this, each major linkage is examined in turn and cause-effect matrices are constructed. Where possible, approximate graphical or mathematical relationships are established. The designer will have to take the lead here in suggesting possibilities and filling in gaps where necessary. When preliminary agreement is reached these relationships can be built into a prototype program as quickly as possible to produce a 'draft' set of results which can be demonstrated to clients and suitable revisions made. The whole process is repeated a number of times and extended to other parts of the model. Turning the relationships discovered so far into the kind of mathematical language which is necessary requires mathematical skills which are not appropriate to cover here in detail, but a few simple examples will be given. The interested reader is referred to the journal *Simulation and Gaming* for a selection of articles on the kind of mathematical functions that have been found useful.

Let us take a simple example in which the quantity demanded for a particular product (Q) depends on two values, both of which are decided by a team. Let these be the unit price of the product (P) and advertising expenditure (A). A simple form of mathematical function is developed by assuming that the impacts of both price and marketing are independent of one another, thus:

$$Q = a + b \times A - c \times P$$

where a, b and c are constants. Note that an increase in price P will decrease demand Q due to the negative sign of c. The amount of decrease in Q due to a unit increase in P is defined by the value of c. Similarly, the amount of increase in Q given by an increase in A is defined by the value of b. The disadvantage of this simple formula is that the effect of a unit change in P (the 'price elasticity') is the same no matter what value P has. This would be unrealistic in many situations where the price elasticity would depend on the value of the price.

Similarly, the above formula does not allow for the effect of advertising to vary. It would be quite usual to expect that low values of advertising expenditure would have a low effect on demand for a product, but as advertising increases then the message becomes memorable and so the effect increases. This continues up to a certain point, beyond which customers may become bored with the message, at which time the effect begins to saturate, as shown in Figure 5.10.

In order to represent the shape shown in Figure 5.10 we need a non-linear relationship, often represented by the following type of formula:

$$Q = (a + b \times A^b)/P^c$$

where A is raised to the power of constant b, and P is raised to the power of constant c. Many other forms of relationship are possible and

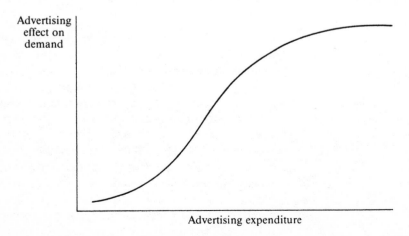

Figure 5.10   *The effect of advertising on demand*

great care is necessary to develop one which responds to all possible decision values in the desired way.

In addition to marketing issues, personnel matters will also be modelled in a similar way, for example to establish the relationships governing productivity and morale.

Operational and financial aspects

The operational part of the simulation will show, for example, how the production system works, and how related activities like purchasing and personnel matters can be modelled. The difficulties will usually concern questions of detail, and how much to include or leave out of the simulation without destroying its purpose. There will also need to be clear agreement on the limits to each of the decision variables that have been agreed, and any combinations of them which are considered unfeasible.

There will also be a number of points in the model which have financial implications. In many cases it will be much easier to model the income-generating side of the business than to model the cost elements. So the focus will be upon scrutinizing cost issues in detail, with reference to real data wherever possible. The design of the financial part of the simulation is essentially much the same whatever the detailed design of the behavioural or operational parts of the simulation. The financial structure usually follows the flow of events and resources. A distinction must also be drawn between cash and profits, as in reality. This means among other things that the time delays involved in income and cost streams must be included. For these reasons it is usually advisable to have an accountant as part of the design team.

6 Programming the simulation

It is not appropriate to discuss programming techniques in detail here, but we may note a number of new developments which are relevant to simulation design. Simulations have been written in a wide variety of languages, including well-established ones such as BASIC or Fortran. Other newer languages such as C or Pascal have also been used and these can offer higher quality screen displays and graphics. Almost any computer language can be used, including spreadsheets for simpler simulations. The example in the next chapter is written in Lotus 123. Spreadsheets do not offer the greatest visual appeal, but they do have the advantage of transparency. Users are able to see the complete structure of the simulation and the data used, which is not nearly as easy in other languages.

The operational simulations described in Chapters 2 and 3 are usually written in purpose-built languages such as Witness (Istel) or Simula. Witness is a highly sophisticated visual system being simulated on the computer screen. This helps the manager to understand and accept the simulation results. Simula is a very flexible language but without the statistics or animation.

Recently a number of new packages have been developed which include some of the features of visual simulation languages and are suitable for use in various stages of business simulation development.

COPE (Bath Software) offers an influence diagram facility which may be used to develop the kind of diagram shown in Figure 5.7 above. It allows users to explore and analyse the implications of such diagrams and shows how one event can affect another. It does not, however, provide the facilities to construct the final simulation programme. A similar piece of software GAMMA (Unicom), now available in English, also provides a way of drawing simple influence diagrams and is an ideal way of facilitating simulation design.

A piece of software which combines the appeal of visual model building with the power to construct simple numerical models is IThink. The user can construct the influence diagram on screen and also specify the type and strength of each relationship.

Prototyping   Whatever computing language is used, the prototyping approach must be employed. This approach is designed to develop a quick, inexpensive 'experimental' version of the simulation in the expectation that the prototype will quickly be superseded by later and better versions. Figure 5.11 contrasts the traditional and prototyping approaches to program development.

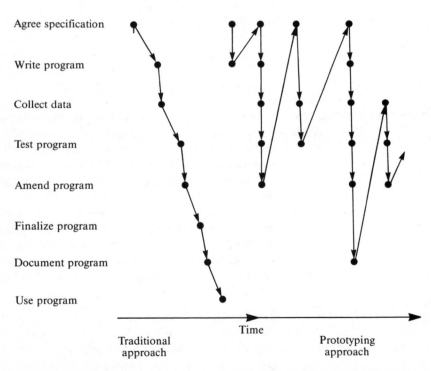

Figure 5.11   *Traditional and prototyping approaches to program development*

Thus the various steps in programming, and indeed in the whole design process, occur in rapid sequence, often overlapping one with another. It is far better to complete part of the design work and get the resultant partial model working quickly, than to spend weeks or months designing a complete model in isolation from the client. Although the prototyping methodology seems more time-consuming, it has the major virtue of keeping the client fully involved and gives him or her more opportunity to influence simulation design and therefore feel a genuine commitment to the final product. This is why prototyping leads to a satisfactory simulation more quickly than the 'traditional' approach. The latter may often require major and time-consuming revision at a relatively late stage in the process. The prototyping approach is generally most useful where programming requirements are relatively unstructured, and where less scientific and more 'political' approaches have to be used, which is the case in simulation design (Boar, 1984). By using this approach, the designer will also learn more about what the client needs, and the whole approach will lead to a great deal of interaction between the user and the designer throughout the design process.

Data collection   This is an essential stage of the design process. The amount of data will have been determined by the previous stages in the design. In some cases, according to the degree of abstraction employed in the simulation, real data must be used, say on sales volumes, unit costs, or pay scales. In other cases, because the simulation involves simplifications or for reasons of confidentiality, it will be necessary to collect representative or simplified data. This should present no difficulty, particularly if those needed to provide the data have been part of the design process.

7 Testing and validation

The simulation is never complete just because the program is finished No designer can ever predict the behaviour of teams when taking part in the simulation so he or she will have to wait to see what happens in practice when the simulation has been used a few times. Some changes will inevitably be necessary in the light of the experience gained from using the simulation, and the designer will do well to take careful note of the comments made during the first few runs of the simulation.

Credibility   The question of credibility can take many forms. One is the question of whether or not the conditions that arise in the simulation could happen in the real world. This is difficult since simulations allow the exploration of a far wider range of alternatives than is possible in real life, in fact they are often deliberately designed for this purpose. Under these conditions it is hardly fair to say that 'it would never happen that way in the real world'.

Here we have to examine carefully the economic and market conditions that were prevailing at the time, and the actions taken by teams. The economic conditions might well have been ones which have never been encountered before, but were they totally inconceivable? Were they the kind of conditions that might happen in the future, about which the organization concerned would do well to consider a suitable reaction? We may then consider the actions that were taken by each team. Were these wise under the circumstances? Were they perhaps influenced by encountering business conditions which had not been met before? With hindsight, was there a better set of responses that might have been made? Did the team(s) concerned actually make matters worse by responding unwisely?

A well-designed simulation will take participants into areas which they have not experienced before, but a careful interpretation of results will usually show them to be credible. The most powerful test of credibility is therefore not whether those conditions could occur in reality, but whether or not the results themselves are logically valid and consistent. This is partly the simple matter of determining whether the simulation model is accurate, i.e. whether the 'sums' work, and partly whether results can be shown to arise from the prevailing conditions and decisions taken.

An example occurred during a recent conversation between the finance director of a prominent UK company and the designer of a simulation tailor-made for the company. They were reviewing the results of the simulation which had recently been run. The finance director looked at the financial results achieved by the three teams who had taken part in the simulation and agreed that most were realistic. One or two figures were, however, a little unusual, and the designer pointed out that this was inevitable, since the simulation positively encouraged teams to explore new avenues. To allow an appropriate degree of freedom of action therefore meant they would sometimes achieve new and different results. Therefore, the most important test of credibility is whether or not the design team, and particularly the intended participants, find the exercise believable and useful, and whether it achieves its purpose.

The program must at some stage be thoroughly tested using real data. In terms of the results achieved, it is best to aim for results which show a robust response to all major decisions rather than precise accuracy compared with reality. Figure 5.12 shows the steps to be taken in testing the simulation.

Initial stages of testing will be done by the designer alone, and progressively more people will be involved in the process, until it is robust enough for general use. We can validate the accuracy of certain parts of the model very easily, especially those built around purely logical or financial relationships. This will usually be done at an early stage by the designer or design team. There is no substitute for real-life testing. It is essential that the simulation is tried out by a group who are as similar to the intended participants as possible. They will often uncover inconsistencies in the simulation or in the documentation. For major simulations it is usual to run several trials with a sympathetic audience before trying it out with the intended participants, making modifications and improvements to the documentation and program throughout. This is not to say that mistakes have necessarily been made by their design team, but that they have perhaps been too close to the project and need other opinions from others who know the subject but who have not been so close.

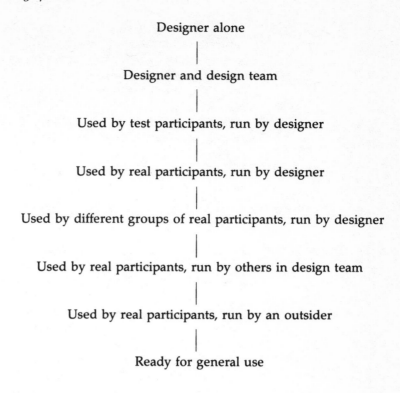

Designer alone

|

Designer and design team

|

Used by test participants, run by designer

|

Used by real participants, run by designer

|

Used by different groups of real participants, run by designer

|

Used by real participants, run by others in design team

|

Used by real participants, run by an outsider

|

Ready for general use

Figure 5.12   *Testing a simulation*

The simulation must therefore pass through a sequence of increasingly more stringent tests as shown in Figure 5.12. Most of these will need to be repeated several times, especially when the simulation is run by people other than the designer.

Preparing the simula-
tion for others to run

It is one thing to finish a simulation which can be successfully run by the designer, or even by one of the design team with the designer present. It is quite a different matter to ensure that the program and documentation are foolproof enough for anyone else to use them successfully. Any programmer will know that it is usually straightforward to write a program to be run only by the person who wrote it. It is much more difficult to develop a program which can be run by anyone else. In this chapter we cannot hope to deal with this topic thoroughly, but we will attempt to give a few insights into why this can be so difficult and what can be done to overcome some of the problems.

The question of preparing the simulation for others may arise at the outset, particularly if the designer has been commissioned to produce the simulation for wide circulation. On the other hand, the question may only arise after a simulation has been designed for a particular use and found to be of wider appeal. In either case it is clearly vital that the simulation has been very thoroughly tested before it is used, particularly by others not involved in the design process, as shown in Figure 5.12.

The program must be designed to deal with every conceivable input by the user, including those which are logically invalid. This means that the program must have a comprehensive set of error-trapping routines to prevent invalid decisions or other inputs. It must also take the user step by step through the processes necessary to produce results. Documentation, whether part of the software itself or written separately, must also show how to run the program under all possible conditions. The documentation should be sufficiently detailed to contain advice on all the many factors that need to be taken into consideration, many of which will be well known and so obvious to the designers that the designer may find difficulty in spelling them out. This makes it essential that those not connected with the design should be allowed to test the simulation and documentation.

8 Documentation

The amount and type of documentation required will largely depend on the way in which the simulation is being used. Generally there are two types of documentation, for administrators, and for participants.

For administrators

The amount of documentation will depend on who is going to run the simulation. For example, if the designer will be wholly responsible there will be little need for any documentation at all. If, on the other hand, the simulation is being designed for others to use then literally every aspect of the simulation must be explained. The following major headings in the administrator's guide should include:

- advice on appropriate audience, minimum and maximum number of teams, team size and constitution
- knowledge and previous experience required by participants
- detailed notes on points to cover in briefing and debriefing sessions, including advice where necessary on how to judge teams' performances, and the conditions under which the administrator should intervene and give advice
- a typical timetable of events during the simulation, i.e. how long should be allowed for each decision period
- advice on how to deal with any conflicts or disagreements that may arise
- an explanation of how the simulation works, and the assumptions underlying it, including appropriate graphs or diagrams. This must, of course, be intelligible to anyone who has not been involved in the design process and who may have no detailed knowledge of the subject matter
- a detailed step-by-step guide on how to run the program, and what to do if something goes wrong
- a similar guide on how to run any ancillary programs, for example spreadsheets, summary programs, etc.

For participants

- The participant's guide should explain the overall purpose and background to the simulation, the 'ground rules', the set of decisions that are required, and what roles and procedures are necessary. Any deliberate departures from reality and major simplifications of the simulation should be explained and examples of the results given, together with a full explanation of any terms used and how they are produced.

- Supplementary information to be issued from time to time to explain any unusual or additional features of the simulation.
- Market surveys or similar information for which a charge may be made. These must be reasonably accurate, which is not too difficult a task since the simulation designer usually has full powers of 'precognition', having run the simulation before.
- Descriptive material showing how to use any additional models, or how to enter decisions into a computer (if appropriate).
- Pro forma sheets (if appropriate) for the calculation of possible results, if no 'what if?' model is available. This is important if the result of miscalculating the consequence of decisions is potentially disastrous on the team's financial position in the next period.
- Decision sheets (if appropriate) for the team to enter decisions and pass them to the simulation administrator.
- Objectives sheets (if appropriate) for teams to specify their own corporate or personal objectives.

9 Developing the simulation

Even when the simulation has been designed and successfully used for a period of time, continued work is necessary to keep it up to date. A worthwhile simulation is a living thing. If it is going to remain useful over an extended period of time it must change as the real conditions upon which it is based change. This means that as significant new economic or business conditions arise these must be incorporated into the simulation. If appropriate steps were taken at the design stages this should be possible without fundamental design changes. Participants' reactions should also be monitored regularly as these are a useful source of ideas for improvement. The design team should, therefore, meet at regular intervals to ensure that any necessary changes and improvements take place.

References and addresses

Bath Software Research Ltd, 40 Park Street, Bristol, BS1 5JG.

Boar, B. H., 1984 *Application Prototyping*, Wiley, New York.

Coyle, R. G., 1977 *Management Systems Dynamics*, Wiley.

Eden, J., Jones, S. and Sims, D., 1979 *Thinking in Organisations*, Macmillan.

Hammond, J. S., March/April 1974 'Some Do's and Dont's of Computer Models for Planning' in *Harvard Business Review*, pp. 110–23.

IThink, High Performance Systems Inc, 45 Lyme Road, Hanover 03755, USA.

Istel Visual Interactive Systems, Highfield House, Headless Cross Drive, Redditch, Worcs, B97 5EQ.

Moore, C. M., 1987 *Group Techniques for Idea Building*, Sage, California.

Simula a.s., PO Box 4403, Torshov, N-0402, Oslo 4, Norway.

Unicom Management Systems GmbH, Postfach 1403, D-7758, Meersburg, Germany.

6 An example design—Stoke Mandeville Furniture

This chapter shows how to design a simple business simulation. The example is fictitious but is based upon a number of real simulations designed by the author, particularly those dealing with small businesses. The designs involved discussions with owners of the businesses and with accountants advising them. The simulation will be called Stoke Mandeville Furniture (SMF). SMF is based upon a small company that manufactures and sells a range of garden furniture of both traditional and modern design. The business is owned and managed by the family.

The chapter describes the major issues facing SMF and the various stages of simulation design. The development of the simulation is illustrated using a variety of diagrams and graphs. Readers wishing to know more about how the simulation works are referred to Appendix 1, which includes documentation for SMF and gives more details of the market and employee-related issues which are central to SMF.

Stoke Mandeville Furniture

SMF was founded several years ago and occupies a large piece of land on the outskirts of a town in the home counties. Initial discussion with the owners centred around the kind of problems and issues the company faced. These were typical of the problems faced by most small manufacturing businesses and are summarized below:

1 A continuing concern was how to develop the awareness and reputation of the company and its products in the local market. This, of course, depends on who and what constitutes the local market. The owners had no ambition to market their products nationally nor compete with nationally-known garden furniture manufacturers or suppliers. Their customers were mainly private individuals and retailers from the local area, which was defined roughly as those people living in a 30km radius of the company.

2 Dealing with inflation and high interest rates were naturally concerns. For this reason, both interest rates and inflation rates were explicitly included in the simulation, both being under the control of the administrator.

3 An inevitable result of high interest rates was the need to control cash flow. Despite having been in existence for several years, the company was still operating with a large overdraft and a loan and was therefore particularly vulnerable to interest rate fluctuations. In the long term the owners were anxious to pay off their overdraft and loan and become fully independent.

4 Keeping employees was not easy. Most jobs were not highly skilled, and supervision was carried out by family members or by senior, experienced employees. Despite high unemployment the company found that many employees did not stay more than a year or two. Although it was fairly easy to recruit new employees, recruitment and training took several months.

5 Seasonality was a recurring difficulty in this type of business. The demand for garden furniture was high in the spring and summer months and low in the winter. This led to the dilemma of whether to continue manufacturing throughout the year, stock-piling for the summer months, or whether to reduce production and possibly lay off employees in the low season in the hope of building up staff and stocks again in the spring. Fortunately, the production process was simple and production lead times were short.

6 Partly arising from the seasonality problem, there was a problem of keeping an appropriate balance between supply and demand. This applied most obviously to finished products, since the company wished to offer customers immediate delivery from stock or delivery within a short time of order placement. On the other hand, the owners were well aware of the dangers of overstocking. The supply and demand balance also applied to raw materials, which had to be ordered in advance. The other vital resource was employees and here too an appropriately sized workforce had to be employed throughout the year. One way of dealing with fluctuating demand was to use overtime in high season. This was expensive but popular among employees.

The production process

Products were made to a high quality and constructed from a variety of timber, both hardwood and softwood, and from metal and plastic components. Timber and metal products were constructed on the premises from standard raw materials, using a range of wood-working and metal-working equipment. Furniture was sometimes sold to customers for self-assembly. Plastic furniture was currently bought from suppliers and retailed directly to customers.

Raw materials were therefore simple and most were available immediately or within a few weeks, except some metal and plastic components which could sometimes take several months to arrive after an order. The tools and equipment used in production were simple and reliable.

Products

The company sold a range of products varying from traditional timber or metal garden chairs and tables, to modern plastic ones, and a variety of other garden accessories. In order to capture the full range of issues and problems mentioned above without undue complexity, it was decided to concentrate on a single 'product' selling at around £700 per item, which corresponded to a typical order size.

Display and delivery   The owners were fortunate to possess a large piece of land, part of which was devoted to a permanent display of goods of all types. This display area was considered to be a good selling point for the company, as it gave customers a good impression of how the furniture looked in a realistic setting. It was also thought to be important to offer free delivery for customers who bought a certain value of goods. In practice, this applied to most customers, since few were able to take their own purchases home.

The market   Geographically, the company was situated some 40 km from London and customers usually came from within a 30 km radius. Customers got to hear about the company either by word of mouth, or from seeing advertisements in local media. The market contained some first-time buyers and some buyers who were replacing existing furniture. Timber-based products only have a limited lifetime, particularly since most purchasers do not maintain them adequately. The more recent plastic-based products last longer, but can get damaged and there was thought to be a small but growing replacement market for these too.

Current sales were around 50 units per quarter (i.e. 50 sets of furniture each worth around £700), although this varied strongly due to seasonal effects. It was thought that potentially sales could increase by 20 or 30 per cent over the next two years. Several factors influence the actual as opposed to the potential sales. The first was the awareness of the company among potential customers. This was achieved mainly through local advertising in newspapers, radio and hoardings. It was felt that currently awareness was low, perhaps around the 25 per cent level only. Realistically, awareness would never approach 100 per cent using these methods, but significant improvements could obviously be made. More important than awareness was the perceptions among customers of the quality of products, and the speed of supply. The owners felt that what customers valued most were:

- quality of finished products
- availability of products either from stock, or within a few days or weeks of order
- free delivery of orders above a certain size
- price relative to inflation rather than in comparison with other suppliers, since there were few other suppliers and in any case it appeared that customers did not usually 'shop around'
- a good display of finished products—this made it important to keep a display of goods covering the whole range of products on display, so that customers could actually see and try out products before purchasing
- the courtesy and product knowledge of staff

After discussion, and in the interests of simplicity, it was agreed that the major factors influencing the buying process were price in comparison with inflation, and availability of supplies.

Employees   Seven semi-skilled employees were engaged in the production and assembly of furniture. The company generally employed young untrained or part-trained school leavers, and inevitably found it hard to pay them well enough to avoid fairly high natural turnover, despite fairly high levels of unemployment. Pay levels were fair compared with similar employers, but not sufficient to keep young people for long periods. Employees typically came from school or from another job at the age of 16 to 18, and stayed for a year or two. During their first few months they were given basic training in wood-working and metal-working skills, usually from one of the owners or from the longer-term employees who enjoyed passing on their expertise.

The average cost of hiring and training a new employee could be equated to one month's pay. New employees were often available almost immediately, but did not become fully effective for a couple of months. The owners wished to treat employees as well as possible and offer good conditions of employment. Even if facing an economic down-turn and the business suffered a severe decrease in orders, they wished to avoid any redundancies and any staff made redundant would receive three months' notice and one month's pay.

Designing the simulation

Participants   The simulation was designed to be used as a simple illustration of the kind of problems which many small businesses face. It may be used in secondary or higher education, or for anyone needing an improved business or financial awareness, particularly within the context of small businesses. The simulation is simplified in many respects, and many financial, production, marketing and personnel details are omitted. However, many important issues facing all small businesses are illustrated, including the need to promote the company and its products, deliver a high quality product, keep employees and bankers happy and endeavour to be profitable. These aims have to be achieved in the face of cash flow difficulties, seasonality, high interest charges and an uncertain economic climate.

Purpose   The purpose of the SMF simulation is to provide a simple but typical illustration of the kind of problems which many small businesses face. The final product is one which can be used in secondary or higher education, to develop enhanced business and financial awareness.

The simulation was designed to be played by teams or by individuals, each team having access to its own computer. The software provides no interaction between teams and the simulation is provided with full participant and administrator documentation. Examples of both the participants' and administrators' guides are contained within Appendix 1.

Timescale   In order to capture the seasonality of the business and include issues relating to raw material supply and employee recruitment, the most appropriate time period was a quarter. The simulation provides the results of the first four quarters and allows participants to run the firm for the next eight quarters.

Decisions   The number and type of decisions were a compromise. The owners of SMF found themselves involved in an enormous range of duties from day to day. Some of these were essential to the effective running of the business, and, as they admitted, some things were done because they liked doing them. After consideration, the following were considered the essential quarterly decisions needed to run the company:

1 *Production units*—the number of finished products required to be manufactured.
2 *Selling price* (£s) of products.
3 *Advertising expenditure* (£s) in local media.
4 *Materials units* purchased during the quarter. These would be delivered at the end of the quarter, and hence materials ordered in quarter five would only be usable for production in quarter six.
5 *Employees hired (+) or fired (−)*. Recruitment and training took one quarter, so employees hired in quarter five would only be productive in quarter six. Similarly, staff made redundant in quarter five would be given one quarter's notice and would therefore leave at the end of quarter five. The cost of recruitment or redundancy was equivalent to one month's current basic pay.
6 *Basic pay per quarter*—£ per employee for working normal hours.

Information   A full set of information is available to participants giving the status of
available   the company and its resources. This shows sales and orders, production and stock levels, employee numbers and productivity, and a full set of management accounts, including profit and loss statements, balance sheet, cash flow statements and key management and financial ratios.

External factors included inflation and interest rates and the cost of materials and overheads, and these are outside the control of teams. These factors would be controlled by the administrator and would only be revealed to participants one quarter in advance.

The owners of SMF admitted that their accounts were not always up to date, and the accounts shown below were made up by the author after consultation. They represent the business adequately enough for the purpose of the simulation (and probably do so as well as the actual company accounts!).

Essential simplifications

Obviously, a large number of simplifications were necessary in designing the simulation. There was one product type only, involving one type of raw materials. There were no raw material supply difficulties and a constant raw material purchase lead time of one quarter was assumed. The maximum overtime allowed was 25 per cent of normal hours. A constant recruitment time of one quarter was assumed, and one quarter was allowed before staff were made redundant. All employees were assumed to be equally productive.

Seasonality was assumed thus:

Quarter one: January to March	20 per cent of annual demand
Quarter two: April to June	40 per cent
Quarter three: July to September	30 per cent
Quarter four: October to December	10 per cent

All decisions had to be held constant for the duration of a quarter, and all customers paid the same price. Prices were therefore appropriate to the average of retail and trade prices.

If customers were unable to buy what they wanted within the quarter they placed the order, it was assumed that they would wait no longer and go elsewhere. There were therefore no 'back order' arrangements, and any orders not fulfilled in the quarter were lost.

The periods of time to receive payments for goods sold and to pay creditors represented a major problem for the company. Individual customers were encouraged to pay by cash, but most paid by credit card. Trade customers demanded much longer payment terms, and were usually powerful enough to get what they wanted.

After consideration, it was decided to assume that half of the customers paid the quarter after receipt of goods, and half paid the quarter after that. All customers would therefore pay within six months, and there were no bad debts. On the other hand, suppliers insisted on prompt payment terms, usually 60 or 75 days. For simplicity the credit period was set at one quarter (90 days).

It was decided that the best way to represent the cost of delivery of goods to customers was to assume the cost was equivalent to 10 per cent of sales revenue.

Discussions revealed that although the plant and equipment used was generally reliable and needed to be replaced only rarely, it was considered good practice to allow for depreciation over five years, and this is reflected in the accounts. It was decided that overheads would be represented in two ways:

1 A 'fixed' element, to represent heating and lighting, insurance, local taxes and administration costs.
2 A 'variable' element, expressed as a percentage of salaries representing national insurance and other salary-related costs.

The following items of expenditure were outside the control of teams and were linked to inflation: raw material costs, fixed overhead costs, and the percentage of salaries representing variable overheads. The following were within the control of teams: employee pay, prices, and advertising costs. Expenditure on these items should be increased in line with inflation in order to keep their effect constant.

Tax was payable at 30 per cent in the first quarter of each year on the previous year's profits. Losses could be carried forward and offset against future profits. Depreciation of assets was to be allowed against profits, but with no capital allowances. In any case it would not be necessary to purchase new plant and equipment since the existing plant was sufficient for any conceivable production and would not wear out during the period of the simulation.

Design of market model

The techniques to design both the market model and the employee model were very simple, and used the type of tables and charts discussed in Chapter 5. The owners readily took to simple diagrammatic representations such as those shown in Figure 6.1.

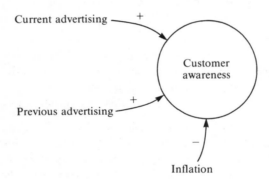

Figure 6.1   An influence diagram of customer awareness

It shows that the major influences on the awareness of the company among customers were both the current and recent levels of expenditure on advertising in local media, relative to inflation. It was thought necessary to advertise regularly, particularly immediately before and during high season to ensure that potential customers were aware of the products at the appropriate time. It became clear that a higher awareness could probably be gained by higher advertising expenditure but since the company could ill-afford to spend much in this way, this was largely speculative, and exactly how much it would cost to gain a substantial increase in awareness was hard to estimate. Figure 6.2 shows the probable shape of the awareness graph. The 'smoothed advertising' referred to in Figure 6.2 implies that the advertising effect depended on the advertising expenditure over several previous quarters, calculated in such a way that most recent advertising had more influence on awareness than earlier advertising. The details of this calculation and the shape of the awareness graph are defined in Appendix 1.

Even at extremely high levels of advertising, it was thought that aware-ness among the general population would be unlikely to exceed 95 per cent. Conversely, 'word of mouth' alone would be sufficient to ensure that a minimum of say 5 per cent of potential purchasers were aware of SMF.

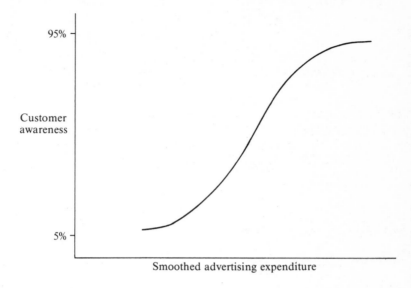

Figure 6.2 *The effect of smoothed advertising expenditure on customer awareness*

Reputation

The two main factors affecting overall reputation were price relative to inflation, and the availability of products on demand. These were thought to be more important if the company succeeded in raising awareness in the local population. Only then would the word 'get round' from satisfied customers that SMF was usually able to deliver from stock or within a short period of placing the order. Figure 6.3 shows the simple influence diagram of reputation, in which price relative to inflation and the proportion of orders fulfilled (in the previous quarter) are both influential in determining the overall reputation.

Figure 6.4 shows the form of relationship thought appropriate for price reputation. This shows that if prices keep exactly in line with average inflation levels, reputation is an arbitrary 25 units out of a maximum of 100. Reducing prices relative to inflation would substantially increase reputation and increasing prices would reduce reputation, but less markedly.

Figure 6.5 shows how the company's reputation for service (i.e. avail-ability of furniture within the quarter that orders are placed) varies with service level (sales as a proportion of orders in the previous quarter), using a simple straight-line relationship.

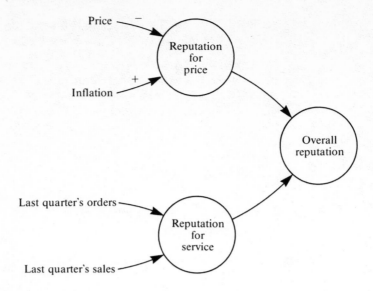

Figure 6.3   *An influence diagram of reputation*

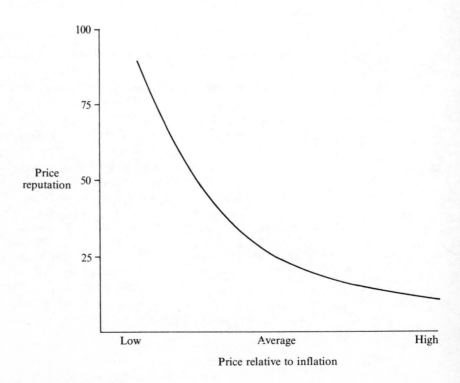

Figure 6.4   *Reputation for price*

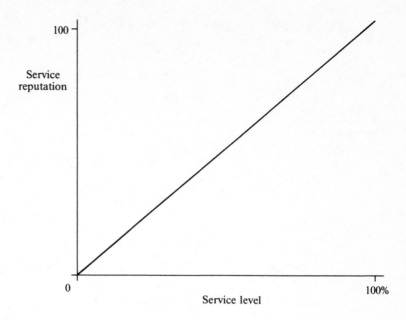

Figure 6.5 *Reputation for service*

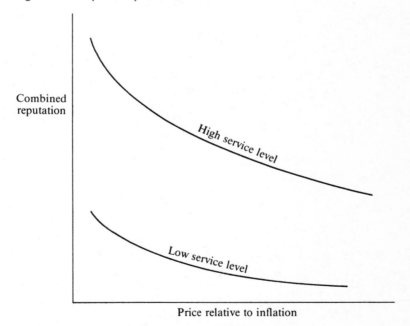

Figure 6.6 *Combined reputation for price and service*

The effects of both price reputation and service reputation on overall reputation were combined, and Figure 6.6 shows a simplified version of the combined relationship. More detailed results are shown in Appendix 1. The number of orders received each quarter were derived as follows:

Orders in quarter = potential market size, allowing for the seasonal
factor × market share.

Market share was defined thus:

awareness of company
× price reputation
× reputation for service in previous quarter

This complete market model is shown in Figure 6.7

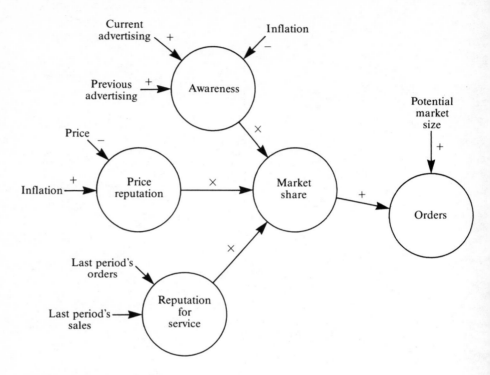

Figure 6.7 *The complete market model*

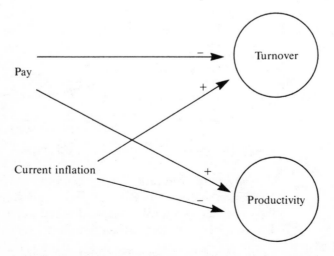

Figure 6.8 *An influence diagram of employee turnover and productivity*

Design of employee model

After careful discussion it was decided that both staff turnover and productivity would depend on pay relative to current inflation levels, as shown in Figure 6.8. Normal staff turnover was known to be fairly high, at about 14 per cent per quarter. After due consideration it was agreed that significantly higher pay would decrease turnover but if pay was only slightly below inflation then turnover would increase dramatically, perhaps by a factor of two or more, as shown in Figure 6.9.

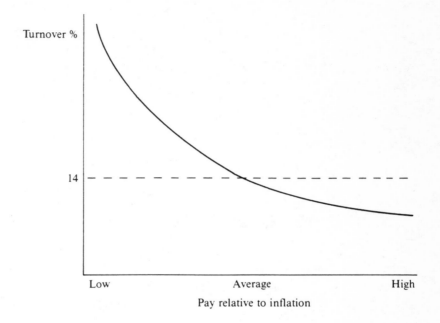

Figure 6.9 Employee turnover

Productivity was thought to show a rather less dramatic variation. Current values were about 15 units of furniture per employee per quarter, and it was thought that changes in pay would only increase or reduce productivity by a few units. Figure 6.10 shows the type of graph used to relate productivity to pay.

Programming the simulation

For simplicity the simulation was developed on a Lotus 123 spreadsheet. The spreadsheet contains decisions and results for quarters one to four and allows users to run the simulation up to quarter twelve. It gives a full set of operational and financial results for each quarter. The layout is described in the participant's guide contained in Appendix 1. The Lotus 123 spreadsheet design made it particularly easy to show progress and made the whole process transparent to the owners of the business.

The only part of the spreadsheet which was hidden from the owners were the mathematical equations necessary to represent the market and employee calculations, and some of the basic data underlying the model. The logic for the calculations is explained in Appendix 1. The

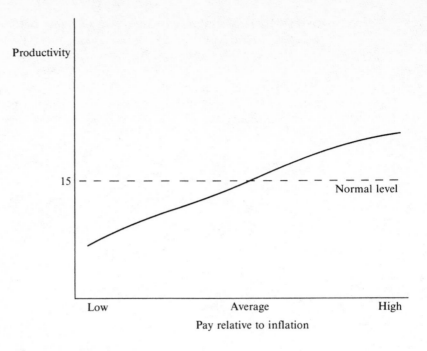

Figure 6.10   Productivity

graphical feature of Lotus 123 provided an ideal medium to demonstrate the graphs used for both awareness and reputation. The effects of
decision and other variables on the shape of the curves could thus be
demonstrated on a separate purpose-built spreadsheet. It is a simple
example, and does not have the most 'user friendly' appearance, having
the usual screen layout consisting of columns and rows.

The participant's guide only refers to the final product, and admits to a
number of simplifications. It also hints at some of the relationships contained in the model and provides enough background to the simulation
for any interested reader to take part in it. However, in order to capitalize
fully on the learning potential, the simulation would ideally be supplemented by additional material either from a trainer or from written
sources. The material would cover general business matters or financial
and marketing issues as required.

7 Running simulations

In many ways running a business simulation is much like running any other training event. Clarity of purpose, good planning, attention to detail and a good dose of common sense will go a long way. However, since simulations are so flexible, they introduce a range of new possibilities and challenges to participants and administrators alike. Simulations can also be more complex to administer than other management training exercises, and they can be run in a number of different ways, as outlined below.

As always, we must start by considering the context and purpose of the simulation, and the needs of the participants. This will hopefully have been done already in the selection or design of the simulation, but when it comes to actually running the simulation then the administrator is as much in the spotlight as the participants and there are many roles for the administrator to master.

The administrator's roles

In Chapter 4 we identified a number of roles that must be fulfilled to ensure the maximum learning from any management learning event. These were shown in Figure 4.2 and will be described now in the specific context of business simulations.

The administrator must decide whether to concentrate on the content of the simulation, for example who 'runs their business best', or who 'makes most money', or on the interpersonal or group processes involved. It is seldom possible for one person to do both. The administrator's personal preferences and abilities will determine which role is fulfilled.

The first role is clearly that of management trainer, whose job it is to provide the necessary enthusiasm for the simulation as a whole and to ensure that it takes place in a supportive and non-threatening environment. He or she will also have to ensure that adequate time is available during the simulation for reflection so that the learning can be consolidated. Simulations can develop a frantic pace of their own as participants become anxious to 'see what happens next'. This tendency for action at the expense of reflection must be resisted.

Another role is that of simulation expert. This entails briefing participants on the purpose and conduct of the simulation, explaining the rules and running the simulation itself. This role will be particularly demanding if using a simulation where changes of parameters such as economic or market trends need to take place. The administrator will need to ensure that changes are reasonable under the circumstances and that participants are able to deal with them. The administrator will also need a certain degree of computing expertise, depending on the particular demands of the simulation. This role will also include that of information provider, in which the administrator will provide market research or additional information at appropriate times. The administrator may also need to be a content expert, to provide any appropriate knowledge input or appropriate models which can be tried out during the simulation. This may involve coaching participants on a range of skills and helping individuals and teams to perform better, either in the context of the task or the interpersonal processes involved.

The final role is that of observer, helping to record participant behaviour and enabling participants to reflect on their experiences at a later date. This is a vital but often neglected aspect of business simulations. This can be a time-consuming activity and if any meaningful behavioural observations are to be made then skilled observers will be necessary, and one observer will usually be required for each group, depending on how much observation participants are able to do for themselves.

Administrators are advised to think through the role(s) they wish to fulfil before running the simulation, and to seek help where a role is required which may be outside their area of expertise. It is almost impossible to give any hard and fast guidelines on how much time each of these roles will take, and the preferred number of administrators that will be necessary in any particular situation. Depending on the physical arrangements, five or more groups taking part in a simulation may necessitate two people to deal with the mechanical aspects of the simulation and help to answer queries in the roles of content expert and information provider.

Preparation

It is vitally important for the administrator to be fully familiar with the simulation. This is easier if the administrator also happens to be the designer. Otherwise it will be necessary for the administrator to familiarize him or herself with the documentary material, and preferably watch an experienced administrator lead the exercise. Taking part in the simulation as a participant is an invaluable way to achieve a 'user's view' of the simulation and find out what types of questions are asked and what are the most common difficulties.

From the designer's point of view it can be very useful to demonstrate a new simulation to a group of colleagues and have them play the part of participants. This has the advantage of showing up any 'bugs' in the software during the development stages and also allows other people to become familiar with a simulation, thus equipping them to administer the simulation when their turn comes.

Team selection

Depending on the purpose of the exercise, it is usually desirable to choose evenly balanced teams. This means that the various different skills and backgrounds within the group of intended participants should be spread around evenly. If there are particular roles requiring special expertise, for example financial knowledge, then this may provide a way of allocating people to teams.

The aim should be to provide for effective and balanced teams, and the Belbin inventory provides insight into how this can be achieved by describing eight key roles that successful teams need to have. If it is possible and appropriate to use the Belbin team roles questionnaire then this will help the job of team selection enormously.

The question of the best number of people to have in a team may be predetermined by the simulation, particularly in the case of a packaged simulation. Otherwise, the best number is linked to the complexity of the simulation, the overall purpose, the time available and the number of participants. As a rough rule of thumb, three people are usually the minimum to engender any team spirit, and any more than six or seven members to a team can make it hard for everyone to participate.

Sometimes it could be more appropriate to allow self-selection of teams, perhaps where other demands for their time make it easier if certain groupings are used. If groups already exist and have been used for other purposes on a course or in the working environment, it may be useful to keep to this grouping to allow teams to get off to a good start on the simulation.

If it is desirable to encourage competition between teams, then three teams is usually the minimum number. The maximum number of teams will usually be set by the simulation itself, or by the physical arrangements possible, for example the number of separate working areas available for team discussion.

Types of use

We now discuss a number of different ways that simulations may be used. The *introductory* or *ice-breaker* approach is one in which the simulation is used as a preliminary to a number of other training activities, or perhaps as an introduction to a complete course. This works well if the participants either know each other already, or have a roughly similar level of knowledge and expertise in the subject matter of the simulation. Sometimes suitably-designed simulations can be used as part of an induction programme for new recruits, introducing them to some of the terminology and issues they will face in their future jobs, and providing an opportunity for an insight into group working. Freeman (1987) describes how a simulation was used for inducting new University students and Gooding (1990) describes how one was used as an introduction for new executive MBA students.

The *skeleton* approach is one in which the simulation is used periodically, perhaps for an hour or two each day of a course, or over a longer period. Other sessions on the course can be used to add the 'flesh' to the bones. These could typically be case studies, readings or discussions covering an issue which is just about to arise in the simulation. This is particularly useful for simulations in which the degree of complexity increases as time proceeds. In this way new features can be introduced at an appropriate time in relation to other sessions.

The *practical example* approach can be used to allow people to practise what they have previously learned. This type of use gives the kind of concrete experience discussed in Chapter 4, giving participants a feel for how financial statements relate to one another and reflect the changing circumstances of a company, and how the dynamics of a particular market work.

The *integrating* approach can be contrasted with the introductory approach described above. This is most commonly the way that simulations are used in management development programmes, particularly those attended by participants who do not know each other before the programme starts. By the end they do know each other and they have had the necessary other inputs to make full use of the simulation. Simulations are often used in this way at the end of a training course as a means of allowing participants to put into practice what they have learned in the course, or to provide a vehicle for integrating together hitherto disparate inputs. The danger is that the 'end of term' spirit can limit the educational value of the exercise.

The *free standing* approach occurs when the simulation is used alone. This is perfectly legitimate provided that the simulation is carefully chosen and run with particular aims in mind. Often this type of use can be employed within a company, using a simulation specially designed for the purpose. The purpose might be to give people in one part of a company an insight into some of the issues faced by managers in other departments, or it might be to introduce a new set of challenges or issues which are thought to be imminent in the real world, in order to provide some warning for the people concerned.

The *remote* type of use occurs typically in a competition which allows participants from many different parts of the country, and from several different countries to take part. Team participants get together periodically in one place and send in their decisions to some central point, often by post.

Running the simulation

One of the drawbacks of simulations is the time they take to run, and this is as true of the initial briefing and final debriefing periods as of the simulation itself. The administrator only has to learn about the simulation

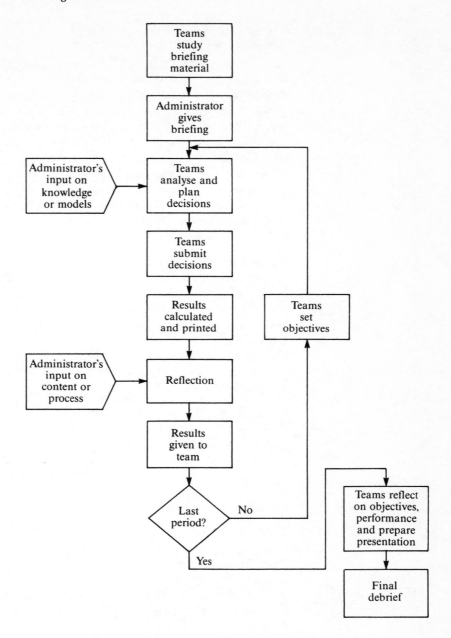

Figure 7.1 *Running a simulation*

once, but each new group of participants has to go through the same learning process to learn about the simulation before they can learn from it.

Figure 7.1 is a flow diagram showing the sequence of events in a typical simulation where the administrator has direct contact with participants.

Pre-reading and briefing

It is often useful for participants to receive the written material describing the simulation in advance, thus allowing them time to do any necessary preliminary work at their own pace. If circumstances permit, discussion of possible tactics can take place in teams, and at this stage it may also be convenient to prepare any trial financial or other statements. Even if a most comprehensive written simulation guide has been prepared there will almost always be a need for an oral briefing, except where this is impossible due to distance. The oral briefing serves several purposes. It ensures that the important points of the simulation are understood fully, and when briefing material is handed out in advance, it helps to ensure that participants who have not read the material as fully as they might have the opportunity to catch up. The briefing also allows for points of administration to be explained, such as the timetable for decision making, practical arrangements, and the nature of the debrief.

It is important to make sure that participants are clear where the simulation starts and stops. There will always be clearly defined limits to the 'reality' of the simulation, and it is far better to explain these at the outset than to let the simulation run for a while, allowing participants to build up plans to do something which is not allowed in the context of the simulation. However, it is impossible to explain everything in the finest detail at this stage and it is preferable to start people working on the simulation fairly soon so that they get involved in learning by doing as soon as possible.

It is best to avoid giving the impression that the objective of the simulation is to 'win' (especially to win at all costs). There will inevitably be an element of competition in some simulations and a degree of competition is desirable, but the main objective is that each individual or team should achieve the learning objectives for the simulation as a whole, and these should be clearly set out in the documentation and in the oral briefing.

The briefing can be greatly assisted by using a set of slides showing the decision form and any other required working forms that will be used. These can be supplemented with a set of informal questions to the participants to test understanding. Experience will tell where participants find any particular difficulties, and a worked example will help to illustrate any potentially tricky point. The aim must be to give participants the feeling that they are about to take part in a demanding but enjoyable exercise. Where the simulation is being used as part of a longer course, then any previous material on the course can be referred to in order to make as many linkages as possible between what has occurred in the past and the simulation. This will help to reduce anxiety among participants.

Analysis and planning

After the simulation briefing is complete teams will return to their own private working areas and begin to plan for the first round. At this stage they may need a fair amount of further help to interpret the rules of the simulation and to be clear about exactly what is and what is not allowed. As far as possible at this early stage, they should be encouraged to set long-term plans and objectives, within which their tactical decisions can be placed. According to the purpose of the simulation and the interests of the particular administrator, teams may be encouraged to set a mission statement showing what kind of team they are and how their overall objectives are to be achieved. Care must be taken during this process to avoid giving an impression that there are 'right' or 'wrong' objectives, and that there is 'one best way' to achieve them. A realistic simulation will allow participants to set a variety of objectives and pursue a multitude of means to achieve them. Some will undoubtedly be more appropriate than others, and objectives will usually be over-ambitious, but this is all part of the learning process. The administrator may need to offer additional input here as discussed below.

Teamwork

There are many ways in which teams can handle simulations, and it is usually advisable that they stop at intervals and discuss the process they are adopting, and whether this could be improved. For example, are there any natural roles arising from the content of the simulation which individuals could fulfil? These might arise from the structure or setting of the simulation and fall along functional lines such as marketing, production or finance. This approach has the benefit that each participant only has to pay detailed attention to one aspect of the simulation. The danger of adopting roles in this way is that the need for coordination and for the resolution of functional disagreements might be overlooked. Often in the early rounds teams will be reluctant to divide up the task in this way, and will seek mutual support in a round-table discussion. Other process issues to be decided include how the team should spend their limited time during the simulation, and how to ensure that all opinions are heard, and agreed decisions made within the timetable.

Decision submission

At the agreed times teams will submit decisions which will be processed by the administrator. This will often produce a short break in the proceedings, which can either be used for refreshments or as an opportunity for teams to carry out further analysis. The administrator will need to pay particular attention to teams' decisions and plans during the first few rounds of the simulation, to ensure that despite the briefing there are no fundamental misunderstandings which will lead to participants making unwise decisions. It can be particularly difficult if a team makes poor early decisions which they have to live with for several periods. In extreme cases a mistake at the start could lead to a situation from which a team may find it impossible to recover. This is obviously very demotivating and the administrator is advised to keep a close watch on early decisions, coaching teams where necessary. The design of the simulation should make this unlikely.

Presentation of results

Depending on the particular arrangements in force, results will be transferred to teams either electronically, perhaps via a network or on a disc, or on paper. The quicker this can be done the better. There may also be a need for less frequent information to be presented in other ways, perhaps by a noticeboard at some central location.

Reflection

One of the most important stages of the simulation is the time required for reflection on the results that have been achieved, as pointed out in Chapter 4. On the other hand, it can be most difficult to 'stop the clock' and ask participants who are anxious to move on to the next round of decisions to give careful thought to what they have achieved and why. One way of achieving this is to ask groups to make a prediction of what they think their key results will be before submitting their decisions. This could, for example, be their market share or sales volume, or their profitability or cash position. After the actual results are known then each team can be deliberately asked to compare their forecast with what actually happened, and try and find the reasons for any discrepancies. The inevitable time delay between submission of decisions and presentation of results can be used for this purpose.

Objective setting

It is useful to ask teams to set their own objectives after a suitable period of time. These can cover whichever areas of the simulation the team thinks most appropriate and the objectives can be as challenging as they feel necessary. This adds to the feeling of 'ownership' of the exercise by the teams. The objectives will also provide a yardstick by which team performances can be compared at the end of the simulation.

Feedback during simulation

If the administrator feels that a team is not approaching the exercise in the best way or is about to make a serious misjudgement than he or she has a difficult problem deciding whether to intervene or not. Depending on the purpose of the simulation, it may be possible to take time out with each team to discuss group processes, or to provide insight into possible cause-effect relationships or simulation rules which the team has overlooked. In the case of a simulation used for team-building purposes, there are usually pre-arranged 'timeouts' during which participants know they will receive feedback from trained observers, and have time to consider how best to improve their teamworking practices. In this context, fairly direct personal feedback can be given where appropriate, and if done in the right way this may be of great benefit to the recipients. Where the purpose is not primarily behavioural, the type and amount of feedback given once the simulation is in progress can be varied appropriately. In the first few decision periods participants are often still struggling to 'learn the ropes', and it is useful if the administrator can be as helpful as time allows in explaining the rules of the simulation, and helping to interpret results. If, however, he or she is asked 'what would be the effect of spending £1000 on advertising in this market, as compared with reducing the selling price by £1' then the answer (even if it is known) will have to be a polite refusal. In any case participants realize they would seldom know the answer to these questions in reality, and the simulation itself will help to throw light on these types of questions. Depending on the extent to which the simulation has been tailor-made for the participants, it may, of course, be part of the simulation purpose to open up just this type of discussion. As time progresses, participants will get to know the mechanics of the simulation and will therefore need less help. They will need an occasional reminder as well as access to any additional information as it becomes available.

As teams get to grips with the basic rules and procedures, the administrator will need to intervene less than in early rounds. Too much intervention could in any case be counter-productive in limiting the experience participants gain in an experiential exercise.

The organization and behaviour of the team and the individuals within it provide an area rich for observation and comment if appropriate and if handled carefully. Most experienced managers will welcome constructive comments along these lines as they recognize that this is the very stuff of the management process. As the cases described in Chapter 8 will show, simulations can provide a very realistic environment for the study of these issues.

It is therefore not difficult to create the atmosphere in which managers expect and welcome comments and insights on their own behaviour. However, to ensure that any feedback is acceptable a few ground rules must be observed, and these will be familiar to trainers. The feedback must be timely so that teams can act upon it, it must be specific to the situation at hand and it must be actionable. This type of activity naturally requires some expertise which some administrators may not feel able to give, and a trainer or behavioural scientist may be essential. If time or resources allow, it can be very useful to discuss with each team the various roles and contributions made by each participant, and how they could have operated more effectively as a team.

Sustaining interest

During the later stages of a simulation some groups may believe they have got to grips with the simulation sufficiently well for decisions to seem routine. In this case it is useful, if the simulation design permits, to introduce some other factors to maintain interest. This can take the form of some unexpected opportunity or threat, for example:

- a real or threatened shortage of supply of key materials or labour
- a real or threatened strike or overtime ban
- a new company entering the industry, acting as a competitor to all teams
- an imposed cost increase or price reduction
- a fire, making operations temporarily impossible at a particular site, or leading to stock losses

In some cases it is possible to introduce face-to-face negotiations, either between a team and a supplier, or between a team and a group representing employees, or between competing teams. Again we have to refer back to the overall purpose of the simulation. Would these additional activities add to the exercise? Would they help to ensure that the objectives are achieved? Indeed would such activities be best carried out instead of the simulation?

There are several difficulties associated with such activities. Firstly they are time-consuming and in order to contribute to the simulation, they must be fully integrated within it. This means that the administrators must organize and monitor this part of the exercise carefully and ensure that outcomes of the negotiations are assessed as objectively as the rest of the simulation. Nothing is more annoying to a team than to spend a great deal of time and effort preparing for and conducting a fruitful negotiation, only to see that their efforts are not reflected in the simulation results. If it is an important part of the simulation to have some degree of face-to-face negotiation, then the administrators must ensure that the results of the negotiation are fairly and objectively assessed, and that the simulation results reflect these in some tangible way.

Debriefing   This is often the most important part of the whole simulation. Depending on the purpose and nature of the simulation, there are several issues to be discussed. It is therefore important that there is adequate time between the end of the 'action' phase of the simulation and the debrief session for proper reflection on results and for teams and the administrator to prepare for the debrief session. It can be useful to ask teams to answer a set of questions during the debrief, such as:

• What were your objectives?
• How did your performance compare with these?
• What particular successes or failures did you have?
• What were your perceptions of competitors?
• How well did you organize yourselves as a team?
• What would you do differently next time?
• What have you learned from the exercise?

During the debrief time must be allocated for discussion and explanation of each team's objectives and progress. It is essential to allow time for each team to speak for itself, in order that they may explain their strategy and progress and to answer the above questions. This is the last chance to ensure that any desired learning points have in fact been absorbed. The presentations can take the form of an annual shareholders' meeting, but care must be exercised to ensure that the presentations, and responses from other members of the audience, do not get too so light-hearted that the opportunity for learning is lost.

In a computer-based simulation there can be a great deal of numerical information to digest at the end of a simulation, often in limited time. For this purpose it can be very useful to have a specially-designed program that summarizes key results so the time during the debrief can be spent exploring questions of how things arose rather than spending time trying to remember or calculate what happened. Many simulations will provide this facility. Some simulations will produce graphs which are useful for summary purposes. It is very helpful if the administrator can keep a note of any particularly unusual events during the simulation.

These notes can form the basis of the administrator's contribution to the debrief session.

Choosing winners

If appropriate, the administrator can choose a winning team, which participants often expect in simulations. There are a variety of methods here, the most popular of which is to choose some overall financial measure, usually profit gained at the end of the simulation. Assuming each team starts with the same conditions and there are no random or other factors which favour one team more than another, then the final profit is indeed an important measure of success. But profit is only one measure of success and it is far more valuable and more realistic to choose a range of criteria. A typical list of criteria for a general business simulation might follow a 'stakeholders' approach as follows:

- treatment of customers—quality of product or service, value for money, level of supply, after-sales service
- relationships with suppliers—the extent to which suppliers have been managed professionally and effectively to give continuity and regularity of supplies at reasonable prices
- approach to bankers and other financial stakeholders—the way any loans have been serviced and repaid
- treatment of employees—general pay and conditions, morale and motivation as evidenced by productivity, labour turnover or any other evidence of disaffection
- treatment of shareholders—share prices, dividends paid, consistency of annual dividends
- financial performance—profitability, liquidity, growth
- achievement of objectives set at an earlier stage
- evidence of learning and improvement in results
- particularly effective teamwork
- use and analysis of information
- the quality of the presentation during the debrief

The final choice of winner using a list of criteria such as these is, of course, far more complex than simply selecting the team that made the most profit. But that is unavoidable if the choice of winner is to be more realistic. Using a longer list of criteria the administrator can, with a little ingenuity, find something good to say about all teams, which is a far better way of finishing any learning exercise, and far more motivating to all teams, than by just choosing a single 'winner'.

Additional inputs

If appropriate it can be useful to introduce short sessions during the course of the simulation to cover points of special interest, or to explain new concepts that are just about to be introduced into the simulation. Also, useful techniques that could be used in the simulation can also be explained, for example sales forecasting techniques or concepts of marginal costing. The administrator can also give inputs on team roles, or suggestions for improved working procedures. Sometimes the proceedings can be stopped for a while to ask a number of pointed questions such as:

Why did that particular problem arise ? How could you avoid it in the future? Put yourself in the position of a potential customer who is considering buying from your company. What are the main considerations that would be in your mind in making the decision? How does your company stack up against these?

These questions can encourage teams to pay more attention to certain special aspects of the simulation.

Decision aids If appropriate, participants can be offered a number of decision aids. The most obvious is a series of pro formas to systematically analyse information or to prepare budgets for the forthcoming period. Often purpose-designed PC spreadsheets can be provided to allow 'what if?' modelling during the simulation. These can form an integral part of the exercise and be supplied along with the simulation on separate discs, or they can involve separate PCs and spreadsheets. Whichever method is used, this facility will provide teams with the same type of computer aids that are available in real life, and it could be one of the learning aims of the simulation to encourage familiarity with such tools. Participants could also be encouraged to develop their own decision-support system using any appropriate software.

Practical arrangements For a simulation to be successful there are a large number of practical arrangements that must be made. Neglecting these vital considerations can lead to disaster. Firstly, it will be necessary, as with any training event, to ensure that a large enough room is available to hold all the participants for the briefing and debriefing sessions. All the necessary overhead projector, computing or similar facilities must be available and working.

Next, having decided the number of teams, it is vital that each team has a private and comfortable room or area in which they can work undisturbed and in privacy. Each room must have adequate table space, chairs, and preferably plenty of flipchart or graph paper and walls that will not be damaged by hanging up the paper. The administrator will also need a 'control room' in which to set up the computer. Ensure there is adequate lighting and power points for computer equipment. Also ensure there are plenty of spare copies of all written materials. Keep backup copies of all discs, not just program discs but discs containing intermediate results of the simulation if appropriate. Ensure that the computing equipment all works and that backup facilities are available in case of breakdown. Spare paper and printer ribbons are essential. If the simulation program does not provide enough copies of documentation for all participants it will be necessary to have the use of a photocopier.

It will also be important to have a convenient central location for the display of messages affecting all teams, for example to show the timetable for decisions, or to present new information or any team results that should be publicly available.

What can go wrong?

There have been a number of cases when simulations have gone badly wrong—usually because insufficient care was taken in briefing participants. In one recent case participants were of a wide variety of different levels of seniority in a company, and the administrator had no say in what their expectations were. They were all rather status-conscious and refused to enter fully into the exercise.

People will naturally resent any situation where they fear they may do badly, particularly if they feel their performance will be known to others who are influential (especially their boss!). So it is essential for participants not to feel threatened. Another common source of problems are technical ones—the computer will not work or the disc is corrupted, or even something as simple as there not being sufficient plugs and sockets to run the computer and printer. The best solution here is prevention. If possible visit the site and try the equipment personally beforehand, arrange for standby equipment, or carry enough spares of anything vital.

What can be done if one team is regularly late presenting their decisions? This only matters in an interactive simulation where it is essential to have all teams' decisions available before they can be processed. This situation must be handled with care, particularly in the first few rounds of a simulation. In any case, it is usually possible to process decisions in any order, allowing slow teams to go last. It is important not to rush things too quickly or the simulation may become a matter of guesswork for some teams. On the other hand, teams that have finished very quickly may have omitted some vital piece of analysis and one of the administrator's jobs is to tactfully suggest that this may be the case.

It is best if possible to keep the timetable flexible for the first few rounds, and gradually speed up as teams gain experience. The ultimate sanction is the threat of either entering the same decisions as last time, or even more severe, for the administrator to enter decisions himself. The secret is to strike a balance offering both fun and learning. This is often not too difficult, but sometimes the balance will tip too far in the direction of 'fun'.

There can often be the tendency to go in for 'endgaming'. Some teams will try and 'go for broke' in the last round of the simulation, often by reducing expenditure on regular items knowing that the end of the simulation is near. Usually players respond to a timely warning that although the end of the simulation is nigh, the end of the world is not! If this fails, a simple sanction is to focus on the extent to which the company is poised for the future, or to adjudicate the exercise up to the penultimate period only.

References

Freeman, J., January 1987 'Computer-based Simulation Games and Induction Training' in *Training Officer*, pp. 18–21.
Gooding, C., 1990 'Introducing Executive MBA Programmes with Management Games' in *Journal of Management Development*, Special Issue, vol. 9, no. 2, pp. 53–60.

8 Case studies

We now present a number of case studies showing how simulations have been used for educational and training purposes. It is, however, a tribute to the realism and flexibility of simulations that they have also been used for research into a range of management and business issues, and the book would not be complete without a description of some of these applications.

Educational applications

The business context
British Aerospace plc (BAe) wanted to use a simulation as part of a training programme for middle managers, from purchasing and supplies areas across the company. The course was aimed at developing their skills as executives in purchasing or materials control positions, and an important element was to place those responsibilities in the wider context of the business as a whole.

The simulation chosen represented the full range of business functions in a manufacturing company, including production, supplies, marketing, finance and personnel matters. After discussion with the company, several improvements were made to the simulation. These included the possibility of raw material supply limitations, to encourage participants to face up to what could happen in reality. Also face-to-face negotiations were an increasingly important element of the participants' jobs, and this feature was therefore also introduced into the simulation. The simulation administrators acted the role of suppliers and time was set aside during the simulation for negotiations. Participants were encouraged to adopt a professional win-win attitude towards suppliers and the quality of their negotiation skills were assessed using agreed criteria.

If negotiations were conducted professionally and a satisfactory agreement was reached, the simulation was designed to reflect this in several important ways. If agreement had been reached on price and terms of supply, then both the unit price of materials bought over the next two or three periods of the simulation and the security of supply would be influenced. Perhaps most importantly, if appropriate terms were agreed, the quality of goods delivered by suppliers could also be influenced. This higher quality was passed on to customers in terms of higher quality finished goods, thus giving teams a clear competitive advantage. The developments brought exactly the kind of results that had been hoped for. The issue of buyer-supplier relationships now figure prominently in the simulation, and the importance of these on other areas of the business was clearly visible. There were obvious financial benefits for those who chose to adopt an appropriate approach to their suppliers, and there were clear marketing and customer benefits too. The simulation also succeeded in showing how decisions in one area of the business had vital implications for many other areas and the need for all departments to work closely together. It also gave a greater understanding of profit and loss and balance sheets.

Development of teamworking skills

Simulations can be used as a realistic vehicle in which to place managers in order to highlight teamworking processes and practices in a vivid and enjoyable way. The detailed content of the simulation is less important than the fact that it offers a realistic task for groups of managers to take part in. Simulations also have the advantage of providing a very clear set of results and performance measures for each team, and the element of competition is often considered important.

In a recent case participants were managers from the distribution division of a prominent motor manufacturer. The simulation involved the marketing and selling of a range of consumer products. Extensive information was provided to each team, which made it important to divide the task between team members. Computer-based decision support and information retrieval systems were also provided as additional features, as similar tools were also used in the managers' real jobs.

The simulation took place over a weekend and the focus of the event was on the roles that various team members adopted, and how each group of managers worked as a team. The simulation was preceded by input on team roles using the Belbin model (Belbin, 1981). There were frequent breaks from the simulation, when the managers were encouraged to reflect on what was happening within their group and their own contribution to the process. These sessions were led by a behavioural scientist who also acted as observer and counsellor. The simulation provided a highly motivating task in which participants genuinely wished to succeed, and which allowed process issues to be discussed. Several lessons were then drawn out of the exercise which could be directly related back to the working situation.

Exploration of business policy

A large multinational research and manufacturing company had a senior manager in charge of each country in which it operates. Each manager naturally had a great deal of autonomy and seldom had the opportunity to mix with their counterparts from other parts of the world. There are therefore great benefits to be gained in encouraging these key managers to get away from their day-to-day jobs and meet together in order to discuss common problems.

The company has organized business strategy conferences for this purpose over the last few years. Company training managers felt there was a need to supplement presentations and discussions with a practical exercise to illustrate some of the current business issues, in particular to illustrate how each country's policies fitted corporate strategy, and how that strategy compared with those of competitors.

For this reason it was decided that a specially-designed business simulation was needed and one was designed which had a number of unusual features. One of its main purposes was to encourage senior managers to see the company through the eyes of their competitors. The simulation was therefore based on the activities of several well-known competing companies in the industry. Each team started the simulation from a totally different position, representing the real-life competitive position of each firm. For example, not all firms were capable of producing all types of product, and had to consider whether they wished to undergo what could be a long and expensive process to develop new products. Other competing firms had already developed a market leadership in some markets, and were therefore able to exploit this position profitably.

A major feature of the simulation was the product research and development process. With appropriate investments in research and development, firms could invent new products. Products then had to undergo an accelerated development and commercial appraisal. When this was complete, teams had to decide whether they wished to market the product. Being first to market a new product could be very expensive but if successful could lead to substantial benefits in the long term. There were also opportunities to enter into agreements with other teams. For example, if one firm had a good reputation in a country, but had no product in a particular market, it could look around for another firm that did have the required product, but perhaps no great presence in the country concerned. If there was such a firm that met these requirements then the potential for an agreement existed. If the teams could forget that they were competitors and strike a mutually agreeable bargain, then there were benefits to be gained for both of them and for customers who needed the product.

As time proceeded, other features of the simulation assumed more importance, including inflation and currency movements. As in reality, inflation occurred at different rates in each country, and the various simulation currencies were subject to their own exchange rate fluctuations. When teams were spending money in one currency and earning income in others, this feature quite naturally attracted serious concern. The geographical territories chosen offered the required variety of conditions, including immediate and long-term sales prospects, credit terms, currency fluctuations, inflation, and import duty.

The simulation encouraged participants to analyse their own company's relative strengths and weaknesses, together with that of their competitors, and to develop appropriate strategies. This led to useful insights into the activities of competitors themselves. The strategies included product development and marketing, geographical and investment policies, and appropriate reactions to changing economic conditions and competitors' actions.

The simulation included enough reality and challenge to keep all the participants fully involved. It was a highly stimulating and compelling exercise which compressed several years' experience into a few hours, and brought to the surface the key strategic issues for which it was designed.

Hospital training

Several simulations have been developed to help train hospital administrators. The simulations can have several purposes. They may be used at the hospital design stage to help decide how to allocate funds between different facilities (i.e. as an operational simulation), or they may be used to help train managers or clinicians responsible for the day-to-day running of the hospital (i.e. as a 'business' simulation). The simulations are often based on an actual hospital, with data relating to the numbers of patients and patient length-of-stay and measures of well-being. Patients can require either emegency and non-emergency treatment (for a typical example see Knots *et al*, 1990, or Trappl, 1988).

When used as an educational device participants are invited to choose a number of targets from a set of targets which are often mutually incompatible. They make decisions in order to achieve their objectives, subject to cost and other constraints. The decisions typically refer to the numbers of employees of various categories in each department, overtime working, increases of patient stay beyond accepted minimum times, and expenditure on equipment and research and development. Other issues might include the allocation of beds to different categories of patients and a range of different ways of managing the required workload. Participants can have the power to do things which they would be unable to do in reality. High expenditure on research and development attracts highly qualified physicians which enhances the reputation of the hospital, but which reduces the funds available for other purposes.

The results of the simulations include statistics relating to the health care of patients, such as the length of waiting lists, how long patients stayed in hospital and their condition on leaving hospital. Others include information on the financial status of the hospital and the utilization of staff and resources.

Participants are judged against the targets that they set for themselves and also against other comparable hospitals. The designers point out the importance of the post-game discussion with all groups and the thorough analysis of the results that have been achieved. The discussion then moves on to apply the lessons of the simulation to the real world. Results have shown that participants do not always make decisions in line with the targets they have set. As a result of this type of simulation participants express a better understanding of the decision-making processes in hospitals and how to run a hospital better, including a clearer appreciation of how to plan and allocate resources. Above all they can gain a clearer understanding of the complexity and inter-relatedness of the various issues involved in providing a complex social service of this nature.

Training decision makers in developing countries

In African countries the agriculture and food sectors of the economy play a vital role. Reliable information for planning and taking economic decisions is vital, yet serious problems were noted in the discussions between planners and statisticians. The Harambee simulation (Harambee, 1990) was designed to promote discussion and collaboration between users and producers of statistics in developing countries. Harambee is a fictitious country in sub-saharan Africa and participants act as politicians, planners and statisticians.

Participants have to analyse the social and economic conditions using information provided in the simulation, and they are then presented with a range of typical conflicting priorities and a set of decisions that have to be made. The simulation has been used in Tanzania, Zimbabwe, Rwanda, Mali and Malawi. Designers believe that the results lead to a better understanding of the complex interactions between decisions and their real-world impact, and the importance of the provision of more appropriate information, better suited to users' needs. the aim is also to foster a better understanding between information providers and information users.

Simulating a small business

Most business simulations represent a number of decision periods in which the same set of decisions has to be made each period. This is not necessarily the best setting for a business which is changing rapidly. A recent example involved the design of a simulation in which a number of quite different issues and problems unfolded.

The purpose of the simulation was to illustrate some of the typical problems that small companies have to face in their early years. These include deciding which markets to enter and how fast to expand, dealing with liquidity problems, and the problems that arise when the business is too big for the founder to handle and a more formal organization has to be introduced.

The simulation was based loosely on the affairs of a real company, and each decision period was designed to feature a new problem or opportunity. In addition the simulation naturally featured a range of day-to-day operational issues such as production volumes and prices, wage settlements, how to attract more customers, and many more routine issues. The simulation was designed for the small business and higher educational sectors, runs on a personal computer and is accompanied by extensive documentation.

Administrators can choose which business issues to dwell on, supplementing these with other teaching materials as appropriate. For example, one issue which arises early is the question of whether or not a new product line should be introduced. The company has traded initially in a limited line of products, but it is becoming clear that demand for a new but related type of product is increasing. Teams have to estimate the possible demand for the product and decide whether to invest in the required production equipment. This is a difficult decision since it cannot be reversed. Also staff have to be allocated to the new product, reducing the company's capacity to produce existing products.

At a later stage of the simulation, provided teams have survived the first few years, they find themselves short of factory space. New and suitable premises become available, but they need to finance the purchase of these, and this requires faith in their own ability to continue in business and repay the loan. Also in order to receive the loan they need to develop a business plan in support of a loan application. The trainer can provide additional input and materials at this point, and then run the simulation for the next period, when the need for a loan and the presentation of a business plan will arise. The example simulation described in Chapter 6 is a highly simplified version of this simulation.

Management training for magistrates' clerks

The Magistrates' Courts Service is a local service administered by 105 magistrates' committees, funded 80 per cent by the Home Office and 20 per cent by the local authority. The way in which local magistrates' courts' committees discharge their responsibilities can vary from one committee to another. In addition, the type and quality of information available to each office varies greatly, as does the computer and administrative support available.

The Justices' Clerks are autonomous and are proud of their independence. They have a range of responsibilities, including that of providing legal advice to lay magistrates during a court hearing, training magistrates, and managing the administration of the courts. Justices' Clerks qualify in various ways: they are solicitors or barristers, and may have an arts or social sciences background. They possess excellent verbal skills, but less good analytical and numerical ones.

The recent report into the Magistrates' Courts Service (the Le Vay Scrutiny) investigated many aspects of the service, and proposed a number of options for change. A White Paper was published in February 1992, setting out changes in the way the service is managed. Major proposals include the transfer of the Magistrates' Courts Service to the Lord Chancellor's Department, and a reduction of Magistrates' Courts Committees, with Chief Justices having a legal qualification appointed to each region. This can be seen not only as a further strengthening of the 'managerial culture' within the service, but a re-affirmation of the importance of concerns relating to the administration of justice.

In this context Ashridge Consulting Group were asked to design a new Senior Management Development Programme consisting of a number of modules for Justices' Clerks and other senior staff in the service. The aim was to improve the managerial skills of lawyers and other service staff, and make them more able to take on their new responsibilities. A six-month programme was devised in which groups of Justices' Clerks attended a series of short modules, and in addition conducted project work in the periods between modules.

One major aim was to give participants insight into their own personal strengths and weaknesses, and to enhance their sense of personal empowerment. The first module was therefore an assessment workshop in which participants completed a number of psychometric instruments including the Myers Briggs Type Indicator and the Kolb Learning Style Indicator. Apart from giving participants additional personal insight, this provided them with a means of thinking through their own personal learning needs. The second module focused on the Justices' Clerks prime responsibilities—resource management. The purpose was to give them a 'shock to the system' by putting them into a situation in which they would have to manage an organization by taking account of numerical data. The third module dealt with service and quality issues, the fourth with constraints and cooperation, and the final one provided an opportunity to set personal targets for future training and development. It was felt that a business simulation would be an ideal vehicle for the second module, and a relatively simple one was chosen. It bore no relation to the actual work done by the Justices' Clerks as it was felt that without a great deal of time and effort designing a purpose-built simulation, any simulation purporting to represent the service would be rejected as being unrealistic.

The chosen simulation was one in which performance was not measured simply as a matter of bottom-line profitability. A range of other performance measures were available, including the extent to which each team met the needs of their own customers and staff, and the extent to which they used their own resources wisely. The results showed that even in the simplified context of the simulation, some participants did not fully use the data they had available. The simulation provided the opportunity to discuss how they could improve the way they used data. In order to maximize this advantage, briefings with participants took place before, during and after the simulation, stressing the need to make maximum use of the information available and giving insight into how this could be done. Discussions then took place on how similar improvements could be made back at work.

Feedback from participants was generally positive, and many recognized, perhaps for the first time, that they were not as good at handling numerical data as they might be. Several commented that they had gained new insight into the importance of analysing and using data for decision making.

Behavioural simulations

Looking Glass (Lombardo *et al*, 1976) is perhaps the best known example of a non-computer-based simulation. Looking Glass, described briefly in Chapter 2, has been used extensively as an organizational simulation for various management development activities. The following is a summary of several users' comments.

Looking Glass fully supports the rationale developed in Chapter 4, that managers learn best when they undergo a powerful experience and have the opportunity to reflect on this experience in a supportive and non-threatening environment. By its very nature Looking Glass forces participants to get to grips with unfamiliar situations in a short space of time. Participants only have one day to operate in what is, by definition, a novel environment. In this time they have to be able to exercise a high degree of leadership and judgement, and exhibit a wide range of interpersonal skills (Van Ensor *et al*, 1989, Kaplan, 1986). Managers who have experienced Looking Glass claim they have learned a number of simple but important lessons. These are largely concerned with insights into the nature of managerial work and into their own strengths and weaknesses. They include the importance of appropriate communications at all levels, the need for persistence, the need to avoid undue emotion, and the fact that an organization can be managed without the need for managers to become technical experts.

Criticisms of Looking Glass relate to its very scope. It encompasses so many facets of managerial behaviour that it can scarcely claim to deal with them all. Perhaps it just claims to demonstrate the need for further training or education. This is probably why Looking Glass is often embedded in a longer programme which provides additional material and further skill development sessions where particular needs have been demonstrated. Also some who have played the game do not find the database of responses from US managers to be useful. Looking Glass is also labour intensive, requiring about three or four trainers. It does, however, undoubtedly live up to its name: it provides a mirror for managers to see themselves as others see them, often a salutary experience.

Research applications

Many researchers have found that the reality and relative convenience of simulations make them ideal for a wide range of research purposes (Keys and Wolfe, 1990). Simulations and games have been described as a 'fundamental tool for experimental work' (Bowen, 1978). However, in order that the results are valid the simulations must be properly conducted and the researcher normally exerts a greater degree of control over events than is the case for simulations used for educational purposes. This must be so since the purpose of the exercise is to study people in a particular setting, or undergoing a particular kind of experience. This does not mean, of course, that people are forced into some type of behaviour against their will. If this were the case then the behaviour exhibited would be untypical and this would invalidate the research.

A brief review of some of the methods used in business research will help to place simulations in context. Direct observation is obviously an important way of improving understanding of how people and organizations function, but we do not always have the opportunity to observe the events that interest us. For example, if we wish to study someone's behaviour under a particularly stressful situation then watching the individual may increase the stress. Also the situation we wish to observe may not occur very frequently in the normal course of events.

In some cases a questionnaire may be the most appropriate method of data collection. Questionnaires are particularly useful for gathering information on a large number of people's beliefs or attitudes towards a subject, where direct observation of their behaviour is impossible or inappropriate. Information-gathering interviews are more personal and direct, but of course they take much more time to conduct in reasonable numbers. According to the area of interest, it may be appropriate for people to report on their own behaviour, for example on how they use their time or to understand their contact patterns. Limitations here include the possibility of deliberate bias if people are unwilling to tell the whole truth.

The most reliable research is often conducted in the real setting, but if this is impossible some researchers use a 'laboratory' setting. Often reality is absent since the subjects know they are being studied. The researcher has total control over the conditions of the experiment and can therefore guarantee that the required conditions will occur and that appropriate observations can be made. However, the subjects may fail to cooperate. Simulations and games used for research purposes offer a compromise between the real world and the laboratory. We now examine a few examples.

Team roles One of the best examples of how a business simulation can be used for research purposes is the much-quoted work by Belbin (Belbin, 1981) who conducted extensive research into team performance, using a business simulation, the Executive Management Exercise (EME), played by groups of executives attending courses at Henley College. The exercise appealed to Belbin for a number of reasons. Firstly, team (or 'syndicate') working was the accepted way of working at Henley. Secondly, the outcome of the teamwork was measurable since at the end of the exercise the final asset value of each company was calculated and was a measure of how well or how badly each team had performed. Belbin was able to measure the psychometric profiles of all the individuals taking part, and control the membership of each team. He was also able to study what happened within the teams by means of close observation. He was interested in the relationship between the attributes of the individual participants, the team constitution and the results achieved. Belbin showed that it was not necessarily the team with the 'cleverest' members who succeeded, but a well-balanced team was often the best. From this work he developed his self-perception inventory which indicates which of his nine team roles come most naturally to people.

Belbin was charged with the 'artificiality' of the situation, but made a powerful defence by pointing out the many similarities between the simulation and the managers' real-life responsibilities. The exercise was conducted by around six team members, who had a number of natural roles to fulfil but whose work had to be coordinated. The simulation was interactive, thus team results reflected not only their own decisions but those of their competitors. Companies could buy market research and negotiations took place between each company and other organizations. As he put it:

'What then had the EME in common with the typical problems that confront management teams in practice? It was that departmental interests and decisions had to be balanced and set against the priorities of the business as a whole. Hard data had to be considered along with uncertainty. In effect the EME was all about six people sitting round a table thrashing out problems and trying to make good decisions' (Belbin, 1981, p. 4).

Improving team performance

There have been a number of other approaches to improving the performance of groups in problem-solving tasks, some by unconventional means. Bottger and Yetton felt that most attempts to improve the way that groups performed had focused on group processes, and they wished to test whether or not it would be equally effective to give individuals assistance and advice in problem-solving techniques. They reasoned that individuals often develop inferior solutions to problems because they experienced internal stress which encouraged them to accept or reject a solution without adequate consideration, or panic due to lack of time or resources to tackle the problem properly (Bottger and Yetton, 1987).

The authors conducted research using the Moon Survival exercise, similar to the Desert Survival exercise described in Chapter 2. Performance measures were the same as for Desert Survival, in which individual rankings of items were compared with the expert's ranking. The exercise was one of a series of training activities, and subjects were managers and MBA students working in groups. The groups were divided into two types: the 'untrained' and the 'trained'. Both groups were allowed time to solve the Moon Survival task individually, and then the authors gave the 'trained' groups advice on the possible causes of poor decision making, prior to groups rethinking their answers and solving the problem as a group.

Bottger and Yetton found that the training intervention at the individual level did indeed improve individual performance, as might be expected, but that it also gave improved group performance. This work is a reminder that, while there are undoubtedly a range of 'group' phenomena which occur when teams of people sit down together to solve a problem, the team is still a summation of individuals and therefore team performance can be enhanced by individual development.

The effectiveness of decision-aids

A great deal of attention has been devoted to the development of decision support systems, and substantial claims have been made for them. Several researchers have tried to establish what kind of systems would be most useful and under what conditions. Fripp (1985) used a simple simulation to study whether or not managers would use purpose-built decision support systems and if so what the effects would be on their results.

A simulation was specially designed for this purpose and around one hundred managers took part in it. Several different types of decision support models were made freely available and data was collected unobtrusively on the amount of model usage and the effects of the usage on participants' learning and performance within the simulation.

Decision support consisted of two types of sales forecasting model and a financial model. One of the forecasting models was objective, being based upon the regression analysis of previous results in the simulation, and the other was subjective in that it captured participants' own understanding of how the variables interrelated. Results showed that the majority of managers used the models offered and the subjective model was used most frequently.

One important feature of the research, from the point of view of this book, was that careful measurements were made of how much participants learned about the structure of the simulation they were participating in. The research showed that the opportunity offered by the decision support systems to explore the possible relationships in the simulation were valuable methods of gaining a better understanding of the structure of the simulation. The use of both types of forecasting model gave an important improvement in learning about the exercise.

Sharda (1988) carried out a test of the effectiveness of a computer-based decision support system (DSS) by using a strategy simulation. Senior undergraduate business students, working in groups, played the part of top managers making a wide range of decisions at weekly intervals. Student motivation was ensured by awarding marks depending on group performance in the simulation.

Half of the course was selected to serve as a control group, having no DSS, and the other half was trained in its use and allowed access to it. The DSS in question was based upon a typical, widely available and easily-used commercial system having a spreadsheet format. To use the system, students entered their decisions for the forthcoming period of the simulation, and certain other information. The DSS then produced a series of reports similar to those produced by the simulation itself.

Results showed that the group using the DSS achieved significantly better simulation results, and a smaller variation in results across the playing periods. Groups using the DSS also took rather longer to reach decisions and reported that they investigated more alternatives and felt they had greater confidence in their decisions.

The effects of stress on decision-making processes

Gladstein and Reilly (1985) report on research using a business simulation to study the relationship between the external threats imposed on groups and the decision-making processes used. The simulation was a computer-based business strategy exercise in which groups had to make a wide range of decisions during each simulated period. The simulation also provided for a variety of external events including strikes, terrorist attacks and the imposition of price controls and tariff restrictions, all of which had severe financial effects. At the halfway point in the simulation, the time allowed for groups to arrive at decisions was severely reduced and this feature also acted to increase pressure on groups.

After the simulation, participants' response to the various threats was evaluated by a questionnaire. The questionnaire asked about the amount of information that had been considered during the allotted time period, the perceived level of stress felt by individuals, and the amount of group discussion necessary to reach decisions. Results tended to confirm that under conditions of threat, groups used less information and conducted less discussion than under normal non-threatening conditions. The authors point out that these effects are often ignored in laboratory-based research and that the simulation provided a realistic environment and a sense of involvement making the threats 'real', features often lacking in other types of research.

The above examples show that simulations are very flexible and have been used in a wide variety of circumstances. However, they cannot achieve every learning objective. They are not necessarily the best learning methods under all circumstances and sometimes there may be simpler, quicker or more appropriate methods.

The survey described in Chapter 3 indicated a number of specific ways in which simulations are useful, and pointed out how they could be improved. The need for more closely tailor-made simulations was one of the most often expressed needs. This shows that the days of the general-purpose simulation may be limited, as managers and trainers strive for ever more appropriate and specific learning material.

The 'fear of fun', or the 'trivialization of training' also mentioned in Chapter 3 has been reported before. Some training managers feel that training is a serious business and that training methods used should reflect this. On the other hand, others believe that education can only be effective when 'having fun' is a welcome and normal part of the activity. The secret is to keep the fun and learning elements in balance.

The survey also showed that many of the claims made earlier in this book for simulations are generally supported. These include their realism and the way they offer the opportunity for experiential learning in a relatively risk-free environment. The many research and educational case studies described in this chapter are also testament to their realism.

Ease of use is another major issue. In some cases simulations are run by those who designed them, either from within the company or from an external training establishment or consultancy. In this case the designer will be familiar enough with the simulation for it to present no difficulty. If internal trainers are to become more comfortable with computer-based simulations then it is essential that the simulations are reliable and genuinely user friendly. This will go some way towards removing another fear, that of the need for a great deal of computing expertise among simulation administrators.

If the computing aspects of the simulation are easier to deal with, then the administrator or trainer can concentrate upon the most important aspect of the exercise which is the learning purpose. Simulations provide many excellent learning advantages and the challenge is to harness these advantages to the full.

References

Belbin, R. M., 1981 *Management Teams, Why they Succeed or Fail*, Heinemann.

Bottger, P. C. and Yetton, P. W., 1987 'Improving Group Performance by Training in Individual Problem Solving' in *Journal of Applied Psychology*, vol. 27, no. 4, pp. 651–57.

Bowen, K. C., 1978 *Research Games: An approach to the study of decision processes*, Taylor and Francis.

Fripp, J., 1985 'How Effective are Models?' in *Omega*, vol. 13, no. 1, pp. 19–28.

Gladstein, D. L. and Reilly, N. P., 1985 'Group Decision Making Under Threat: The Tycoon Game' in *Academy of Management Journal*, vol. 28, no. 3, pp. 613–27.

Harambee, a simulation developed in Munich and at the Food Studies Group at Queen Elizabeth House at the University of Oxford. Paper presented at the 6th Planspiel, Bad Neunahr, Germany, November 1990.

Kaplan, R. E., 1986 'What One Manager Learned in Looking Glass, and How He Learned It' in *Journal of Management Development*, vol. 5, no. 4, pp. 36–45.

Keys, J. B. and Wolfe, J., 1990 'The Role of Management Games and Simulations in Education and Research' in *Journal of Management*, vol. 16, no. 2, pp. 307–36.

Knots, U. S., Parrish, L. G. and Shields, C. A., 1990 'Developing Hospital Administrators with the Canadian Hospital Executive Simulation System' in *Journal of Management Development*, Special Issue, vol. 9, no. 2, pp. 22–31.

Lombardo, M., McCall, M. and De Vries, D., 1976 *Looking Glass*, Greensboro. N C. Center for Creative Leadership.

Sharda, R. M., Barr, S. H. and McDonnell, J. C., 1988 'Decision Support System Effectiveness: A Review and an Empirical Test' in *Management Science*, vol. 34, no. 2, pp. 139–59.

Trappl, R. (ed.), 1988 *Cybernetics and Systems*, Kluwer Academic Publishers, pp. 1111–17.

Van Ensor, E., Ruderman, M. and Phillips, A. D., 1989 'The Lessons of Looking Glass' in *Leadership and Organisational Development Journal*, vol. 10, no. 6, pp. 27–31.

Further reading

Specialist books

Elgood, C., 1988 *Handbook of Management Games*, Gower.

A comprehensive coverage of (largely non-computer-based) management games. Gives guidance on the use of a range of such games, but nothing on game design. Includes a directory of (again largely non-computer-based) games, almost all of which are of UK design and focus.

Gentry, J. W. (ed.), 1990 *Guide to Business Gaming and Experiential Learning*, Association of Business Simulation and Experiential Learning (ABSEL), Kogan Page.

This guide provides practical advice on the design and use of a wide range of experiential exercises. It compares several general and functional business simulations.

Greenblat, C. S., 1988 *Designing Games and Simulations: an Illustrated Handbook*, Sage Publications.

One of the very few books focusing on the design of games, but not specifically computer-based ones. Games described cover a wide range of uses including urban planning, business and medical problems. Many examples are given covering a range of social systems, such as marriage counselling, health care, village life and urban policy.

Horn, R. E. and Cleaves, A., 1980 *The Guide to Simulation/Games for Education and Training*, 4th edition, Sage, Beverly-Hills, CA, USA.

A comprehensive, but now somewhat dated guide to a wide variety of games and simulations available in the USA. Includes manual and computer-based simulations, most of which are available through publishers. A fifth edition is to be published shortly.

Jones, K., 1985 *Designing Your own Simulations*, Methuen.

Offers useful advice for the design of simple, non-computer simulations.

Specialist journals

Simulation and Gaming (until recently *Simulation and Games*) is the International Journal of Theory, Design and Research. Edited by C. S. Greenblat. Available through Sage Publications, 6 Bonhill Street, London EC2A.

Simulation and Gaming is the official journal of the Association of Business Simulation and Experiential Learning (ABSEL), the North American Simulation and Gaming Association (NASAGA) and the International

Simulation and Gaming Association (ISAGA). It contains theoretical, research and practical papers related to gaming and simulations, and includes reviews of books and simulations.

Simulation/Games for Learning

The journal of the Society for the Advancement of Games and Simulations in Education and Training (SAGSET), available through the Centre for Extension Studies, University of Loughborough, Loughborough, LE11 3TU.

General publications and articles

Keys, J. B., 1986 'Improving Management Development Through Simulation Gaming' in *Journal of Management Development*, vol. 5, no. 2, pp. 41–50.

Keys, J. B. (ed), 1990 *Management Games and Simulations* in *Journal of Management Development*, Special Issue, vol. 9, no. 2.

Kibbee, J. M., Craft, C. J. and Nanus, B., 1961 *Management Games*, New York, Reinhold.

Klein, R. D. and Fleck, R. A., June 1990 'International Business Simulation/Gaming: An Assessment and Review' in *Simulation and Gaming*, vol. 21, no. 2.

The authors describe and compare four US-designed international business simulations: International Operations (INTOP), Multinational Business Game (MBG), Multinational Management Game (MMG) and Worldwide Simulation Exercise (WISE). They give 13 issues which they contend are important in the teaching of international business, and compare the extent to which the games treat each issue.

Larreche, J.-C. and Gatignon, H., 1977 *MARKSTRAT: A Marketing Strategy Game*, Palo Alto, CA, Scientific Press, and Larreche, J.-C. and Weinstein, D., 1988 *INDUSTRAT: The Strategic Industrial Marketing Simulation*, Englewood Cliffs, NJ, Prentice Hall.

Both the above simulations are very realistic and detailed in the way they treat marketing issues. Both encompass specific market segments in their demand structures. Market shares within each segment depend on standard economic variables such as price and advertising and also on a set of physical attributes belonging to each product.

Rohn, W. E., September 1986 'The Present State and Future Trends in Management Games for Management Development in Germany' in *Simulation and Games*, vol. 17, no. 3, pp. 382–92.

Documentation for the SMF simulation

This appendix contains the *Participant's* and the *Administrator's Guides* for the SMF simulation discussed in Chapter 6. The *Administrator's Guide* explains how the simulation is constructed, particularly in the key areas of customer reputation, market share, productivity and staff turnover. These are the areas of the simulation that usually require most research and are fundamental to the operation of the simulation as a whole. Further information is given on some of the financial aspects of the simulation, and also instructions on how to develop, load and use the spreadsheet. The *Administrator's Guide* discusses some of the ways in which the administrator can change the simulation to suite his or her needs, and suggests how the simulation could be further improved. Any reader wishing to receive a 5.25 inch copy of the spreadsheet should send a cheque for £5.00 to:

Customer Services,
McGraw-Hill Book Company Europe,
Shoppenhangers Road,
Maidenhead,
Berkshire, SL6 2QL
quoting ISBN 0-07-707789-X

When you receive your copy ensure that you take several backup copies of the spreadsheet and keep them in a secure place.

Participant's Guide

This simulation is based upon the activities of a small company manufacturing and selling garden furniture. The company has been disguised, but many of the issues included in the simulation are real enough for all small businesses. You will play the part of the owner(s) of Stoke Mandeville Furniture (SMF), and in the course of the simulation you will be faced with many of the problems real owners of small businesses have to deal with. These include the need to market your products or services, deal with seasonal variations in business, be a good employer, keep within reasonable overdraft limits and run the business profitably.

The simulation is written in a Lotus 123 spreadsheet which contains the results from the first four quarters and all you need to run the business up to quarter twelve. You will have to make a number of decisions, starting with quarter five (January to March in year two). When you have finalized these the spreadsheet will show the full results you have achieved for the quarter and if required these can be printed out for detailed inspection. You can then take your time and analyse the situation carefully before continuing quarter by quarter up to quarter twelve.

Background SMF is situated in the home counties. It was started up a few years ago by the present owner, and specializes in producing a wide range of high quality timber, metal and plastic garden furniture. Most of the manufacturing work is done on site at SMF, by the company's own production staff. The company sells direct to the public and to trade customers who retail to their own customers.

For simplicity, the simulation only represents one type of furniture, but this can be thought of as typical of all furniture sold. Various other simplifications have been made, but the simulation nevertheless represents many challenges which have to be faced in reality.

Decisions Each quarter the following decisions have to be made:

1 *Planned production (units)* This is the number of units of furniture you plan to make in the current quarter. The actual production quantity may be different under certain circumstances (see below).
2 *Materials bought (units)* The amount of raw materials you place on order this quarter, for delivery and use next quarter.
3 *Price (£)* The selling price per unit of furniture. This is the average price received by the company, taking account of discounts offered to trade customers. Generally customers are sensitive to price changes, but will not react adversely to changes which are in line with inflation. You will receive an accurate forecast of inflation before starting each quarter.
4 *Advertising (£)* The amount of money you spend on local advertising each quarter. The advertising is placed in a variety of local media, including newspapers and radio, and is the means by which customers and potential customers are made aware of your company and its products. You therefore believe that it is necessary to keep a regular advertising budget in order to gain maximum benefit. Advertising expenditure should be increased in line with inflation to maintain its effect.
5 *Employees (+ or −)* The number of production employees you wish to hire (+) or make redundant (−) each quarter. It takes one quarter to recruit and train new staff, and in the case of redundancies you always give a quarter's notice. See below for the associated costs of recruitment and redundancy.

6 *Basic pay (£)*   The basic pay per employee per quarter in normal working hours. You do not have to increase pay every quarter, but being a good employer you wish to keep pay at least in line with inflation in the long run. Please note that you will not be allowed to reduce basic pay below half the pay level in quarter one, allowing for inflation since then. For example, suppose that pay in quarter one was £3000 and the inflation index was 100. If the inflation index in say quarter six will be 110 then the minimum pay in quarter six will be 0.5 × £3000 × 110/100 or £1650.

Production   The production of furniture in SMF is a simple process involving traditional skills such as joinery and metal working. There are a number of different styles and types of furniture, but in this simulation only one 'average' type is included. This can be thought of as a set of garden furniture consisting perhaps of a table and chairs, taking a craftsman several days to produce, and costing around £700.

You have a few long-term employees who are trained craftsmen and they take a pride in their work, having been with the company since it started. These are assisted by a number of younger employees, usually school leavers. A range of simple items are used for furniture production, including timber and metal parts and a range of fixing materials. In the simulation these are all represented by a 'unit' of raw material, currently costing about £40 per unit. One unit will produce one 'unit' of furniture. Raw materials have to be ordered in advance, and since you insist on high quality materials, there is no other source of supply at short notice, so you have to ensure that at the beginning of each quarter enough raw material stock is on hand to produce what you want during the quarter.

Having decided in advance of each quarter what your planned production will be, actual production will be determined as follows. If customer demand throughout the quarter exceeds planned production (allowing for the sale of any stock of finished goods made previously), then actual production will be automatically increased to meet the demand, subject to the following constraints:

1 The quantity of raw materials in stock at the end of the previous quarter (i.e. available for use in the current quarter).
2 The maximum production possible by the employees, at their current productivity level, working up to 25 per cent overtime. The critical number is the number of employees you had in the company at the end of the previous quarter, since any new recruits this quarter will not be productive until next quarter.

No increase in planned production is made for reasons other than for high customer demand.

Sometimes customer demand in a quarter will be less than planned production in the quarter, in which case no reduction is made in planned production and you will be able to keep the finished goods in stock until they are sold. This is one of the ways in which you deal with a highly seasonal business, by making more than required in low season and 'stocking up' for high season.

Examples Suppose there are 10 production staff available at the end of the previous quarter and their productivity per employee is 15 units in this quarter. Planned production is 170 units. Assume that 100 units of raw materials are ordered for delivery in this quarter, but will not be available for use until next quarter. Fifteen units of finished goods were in stock at the end of the previous quarter.

The most employees can produce without working overtime is 10 × 15 = 150 units. Working full overtime they can increase their hours by 25 per cent and thus produce 10 × 15 × 1.25 = 188 (rounded).

1 Suppose that raw material stock on hand at the end of the previous quarter was 200 units. Customer demand is 80 units in this quarter.

actual production = 170 (no reduction below planned levels due to low demand, and raw material stocks and employee output are sufficient)
sales = 80
lost orders = 0
closing raw material stock = 200 − 170 + 100 = 130
closing finished goods stock = 15 − 80 + 170 = 105

2 Suppose raw material stock was 200 and customer demand is 210.
maximum production using overtime = 188
actual production = 188 (since raw materials are sufficient)
sales = 188 + 15 = 203
lost orders = 210 − 203 = 7
closing raw material stock = 200 − 188 + 100 = 112
closing finished goods stock = 15 − 203 + 188 = 0

3 Suppose raw material stock was 100 and customer orders are 150.
maximum production without overtime = 150, but raw material stocks do not allow more than 100
actual production = 100
sales = 100 + 15 = 115
lost orders = 150 − 115 = 35
closing raw material stock = 100 − 100 + 100 = 100
closing finished goods stock = 15 − 115 + 100 = 0

Note that you do not need to be concerned about the finished goods stock used for display purposes, as these are produced separately.

Productivity Historically, the company has achieved an average productivity (furniture units made per employee per quarter, working normal hours) of about 15. This is not fixed, however, and will vary from quarter to quarter, being influenced by the pay levels you offer relative to inflation.

You may assume that the quality of the furniture produced does not change, since you offer a good training scheme and use careful supervision. You feel that a substantial increase in pay, if you could afford it, could bring an important increase in productivity, say up to 18 or 20 units per quarter. By the same token, if you let wages slip relative to inflation then despite your best efforts morale would suffer and productivity might fall back a few units.

Being a small local company you have no local competitors and employees do not compare their pay with that of any other company. This means that in the simulation, your employees are not influenced by any other teams' pay.

Customers and markets
The company sells mostly to private buyers and to a lesser extent to retailers. You try to encourage direct sales to private customers and you pride yourself on having one of the best and largest furniture display areas in the locality. This is an attractive feature to most customers who like to see and test the furniture before buying. Bearing in mind your location and catchment area you believe that you can estimate the likely demand for your products reasonably accurately. This is made up from people replacing and improving their furniture, buyers who previously had no garden furniture at all, and a small amount of new customers arising from the building programme in the area. Your advertising campaign and direct selling rely on the fact that your customers tend to come from a fairly small catchment area. You know from analysing the addresses of recent customers that they usually come from a 30 km radius around your factory. The market is seasonal, and you have found that the proportions of annual demand you receive in each quarter are roughly as follows:

Quarter 1 (January to March)   20 per cent
Quarter 2 (April to June)   40 per cent
Quarter 3 (July to September)   30 per cent
Quarter 4 (October to December)   10 per cent

This seasonality is not totally outside your control, since you can to some extent influence customers, by offering price discounts in the low season or by increasing advertising. However, you have not done this in the recent past. The potential market for your products has been estimated at between 4000–5000 units per annum over the next two years, but presently your orders are much lower than this level. Having consulted a friend who has recently completed a marketing training course, you have been advised that there are a number of important factors that must be attended to if you are to increase your business substantially. Expressed simply these mean that you must take steps to make people more aware of your company, and at the same time you must establish a reputation as a reliable supplier of high quality furniture at reasonable prices. The issues of awareness and reputation are now discussed in detail.

Awareness Informal surveys have shown that only around 5 to 7 per cent of potential customers know you exist. You admit this is too low, and the best way to increase it is to increase your advertising budget, but you have felt unable to afford this in the past. In any case any increase in advertising will not produce immediate results and it may take several quarters at the increased level for the full effects to be noticed.

Generally speaking the more you spend on advertising the greater will be the awareness of your company, but unfortunately results are not directly proportional to expenditure. Also, even if most potential customers become aware of the company, the translation of that awareness into an order will usually depend on your reputation as a supplier of furniture.

Reputation There are two key factors here, your ability to supply goods from stock or in a very short time of receiving customer orders and, to a lesser extent, your price. In recent quarters you have been able to deliver 100 per cent of all orders within the quarter that they were placed, and customers have often commented that this is what they value most. This reputation for service is therefore the feature you are determined to maintain in the future. Any customer orders you are not able to fulfil in the quarter are lost, and customers will not return.

Price is also important, particularly for the ability it gives you to slightly reduce the seasonality of the business, which has always been a problem for you. In the long run, you feel it is necessary to keep prices in line with inflation and that generally customers do not resent any such price increases. Any significant increase in price above inflation would undoubtedly reduce customer orders, despite a high level of awareness, and a price reduction would have the opposite effect.

Staff You employ seven staff who are all involved in production. You have no difficulty in recruiting additional staff, but the basic training you insist on means that new staff are not productive for one quarter after being hired. So anyone hired in quarter five would not be useful in production terms until quarter six, although you would have to pay them in quarter five.

Unfortunately, turnover is high, especially among your younger staff. In the recent past turnover has averaged about 14 per cent per quarter, although it could be influenced by pay. A substantial increase in pay, relative to inflation, could reduce this figure a little, but if your pay lagged substantially behind inflation you feel turnover could increase dramatically. You offer overtime payments for a maximum of 25 per cent of 'normal' time. This is, however, no substitute for poor pay since overtime is not guaranteed and is sporadic. The overtime premium is 50 per cent. As an example of overtime cost, consider that you have 10 employees whose productivity in normal working hours is 15 units each. You pay £3000 per quarter.

The maximum amount they can produce per quarter in normal hours is $10 \times 15 = 150$ units, at a salary cost of $10 \times £3000 = £30\ 000$.

If you were to work 10 per cent overtime, this would naturally increase output to $10 \times 15 \times 1.1 = 165$ units. The cost would be $10 \times £3000 = £30\ 000$ in normal hours, and

> 10 per cent $\times$ £30 000 $\times$ overtime premium in overtime hours
> $= 0.1 \times £30\ 000 \times 1.5 = £4500$

So total salary cost $= £34\ 500$.

The cost of hiring and training new employees amounts to one month's pay (i.e. a third of a quarter), and should the need arise to make people redundant (which you would be reluctant to do), the cost will be the same.

Getting familiar with the simulation

To use the simulation you will need a basic knowledge of Lotus 123. Interested readers will be able to construct a copy of the spreadsheet for themselves from the following description. Figure A1.1 shows the layout of all the screens.

C3 Operating instructions	I3
C21 Economic data quarters 1 to 6	I21 Economic data quarters 7 to 12
C39 Decisions	I39 Decisions
C57 Operating results	I57 Operating results
C75 Profit and loss	I75 Profit and loss
C93 Balance sheet	I93 Balance sheet
C111 Sources of cash	I111 Sources of cash
C129 Cash uses and balance	I129 Cash uses and balance
C147 Key ratios	I147 Key ratios

Figure A1.1 Screen layout of SMF simulation

Use PgUp and PgDn to move up and down a screenful at a time, and Ctrl→ or Ctrl← to move right or left a screenful at a time. It is generally easier to move a screenful at a time in this way, and use the up or down and left or right arrows to move a single row or column when entering decisions. Notice that column A has been fixed as titles so that when the screen is moved to the left or right the headings for each row are still visible. Rows one and two have also been fixed to show the quarters one to six and seven to twelve. By using Ctrl← and Ctrl→ you will see that quarters one to six appear on the left hand of each pair of screens (columns C to H), and quarters seven to twelve on the right hand of each pair (columns I to N).

The simulation produces several screens of results as shown in Figure A1.1 These are now described in detail.

Instructions (see Figure A1.2) The spreadsheet should load at this point, showing basic instructions on how to use the simulation. If more than one person or group is using the simulation, and you wish to ensure you can identify your own results, type a name or a team number in cell E3. This will automatically be copied onto other screens.

Economic data (see Figure A1.3) *Seasonality (row 24)*: this is the percentage of annual orders you expect to receive in each quarter.

Loan interest rate (%) (cell C27): the annual interest rate charged on any outstanding loans. The balance sheet (shown below) will tell you what

	A	B	C	D	E	F	G	H
1	SMF.WK1	Quarter	0	1	2	3	4	5	6
2			Press F9 for trial run, Alt M for menu					
3				Team		1		
4	INSTRUCTIONS:							
5			This spreadsheet contains a simulation based					
6	Please read the		upon STOKE MANDEVILLE FURNITURE, a fictitious					
7	Participant's Guide		but typical small company operating with many					
8	first		of the problems facing all small businesses.					
9								
10			See if you make wise decisions and run the					
11			company through two years of varying business					
12			conditions. Can you give customers what they					
13			want, be a good employer, AND make a profit?					
14								
15			Press Alt M to see the main menu. After making					
16			decisions for the next quarter, press F9 for					
17			a trial run, or Alt M to see the menu again.					
18			Select Run from menu to run the simulation and					
19			move on a quarter. Good Luck!					
20								

Figure A1.2 The instructions screen

	A	B	C	D	E	F	G	H
1 SMF.WK1	Quarter	0	1	2	3	4	5	6
2			Press F9 for trial run, Alt M for menu					
21				Team		1		
22 ECONOMIC DATA:								
23								
24 Seasonality			20%	40%	30%	10%	20%	40%
25								
26								
27 Loan interest % pa			10					
28								
29 O/draft interest % pa			14	14	14	14	14	
30 Curr a/c interest % pa			7	7	7	7	7	
31								
32 Inflation index			100	103	105	107	109	
33								
34 Raw material cost £			40	40	41	41	43	
35								
36 Fixed overheads £			3000	3000	3000	3000	3200	
37								
38								

Figure A1.3   *The economic data screen*

loan you have outstanding at any point in time. The cash uses and balance screen (see below) will show the interest you are paying and when you are due to repay any of the loan.

O/draft interest rate (%) (row 29): the annual interest rate you will be charged on your overdraft.

Current account interest rate (%) (row 30): the annual rate you will earn on cash balances.

Inflation index (row 32): at the start of the simulation (quarter one) this was 100. The index for every subsequent quarter shows how much retail price inflation will increase, relative to 100. Thus in quarter two the inflation index was 103, representing a 3 per cent increase over quarter one. In quarter three it was 105, representing a 5 per cent increase over quarter one (and approximately a 2 per cent increase over quarter two).

Raw material cost (£) (row 34): this is the true unit cost of materials in any quarter. Raw materials costs do not necessarily follow the inflation index exactly.

Fixed overheads (£) (row 36): these represent the cost of rent, local taxes and heating and lighting. They are called fixed costs because they do not vary with the amount of business you do.

Decisions (see Figure A1.4)

Planned production (units) (row 41): the number of units of furniture you plan to make.

Materials bought (units) (row 43): the number of units of raw materials you bought.

Price (£) (row 45): selling price per unit of finished goods.

Advertising (£) (row 47): money spent on local advertising.

Employees hired (+) or fired (−) (row 49): a positive number results in employees hired, and a negative number (subject to certain constraints) results in redundancies.

Basic pay (£) (row 51): pay in normal working hours.

Estimated orders (row 54): this feature enables you to do some 'what if?' modelling in advance of committing yourself to final decisions. Note that typical values for orders have been entered for quarters five to twelve. You must enter your own forecast of orders (bearing in mind the decisions you have made, your past results and the present economic conditions). You will then be able to study the predicted financial results. Remember, however, that the accuracy of the financial results depends entirely on the accuracy of your estimated orders. Ensure you set this to zero before running the simulation to calculate the real results.

	A	B	C	D	E	F	G	H
1 SMF.WK1	Quarter	0	1	2	3	4	5	6
2			Press F9 for trial run, Alt M for menu					
39 DECISIONS:			Team		1			
40								
41 Planned prodn (units)			50	60	60	55	NA	NA
42								
43 Matls. bought (units)			60	60	60	50	NA	NA
44								
45 Price £			700	700	700	700	NA	NA
46								
47 Advertising £			500	600	800	1000	NA	NA
48								
49 Employees (+ or −)			1	1	1	1	NA	NA
50								
51 Basic pay £			3000	3000	3000	3000	NA	NA
52								
53 Estimated orders, for								
54 planning purposes. Set			0	0	0	0	50	100
55 0 to run simulation								
56								

Figure A1.4 *The decisions screen*

Operating results (see Figure A1.5)

Productivity (row 58): the average number of units of furniture per employee that your staff were capable of producing in normal working hours. The actual production may, of course, be different from this for a variety of reasons explained above.

Recruits/redundancies (row 59): this is the actual number of recruits or redundancies in the quarter. You will always get the number of recruits you ask for (by entering a positive number in row 49 of the decisions screen), but will not be allowed more redundancies than would reduce your staff below one.

Leavers (row 60): the number of staff who left the company voluntarily during the quarter.

Employees (end qtr) (row 61): the number of employees you have at the end of each quarter, taking account of the number you had at the end of the previous quarter, any voluntary leavers, and your hiring/firing decision. You must always keep at least one employee.

Actual production (row 62): the amount of production you actually achieved in the quarter, subject to the considerations explained above. This is the total production in both normal and overtime hours.

Overtime production (row 63): the amount of production achieved in overtime (if any).

	A	B	C	D	E	F	G	H
1	SMF.WK1	Quarter 0	1	2	3	4	5	6
2			Press F9 for trial run, Alt M for menu					
57	OPERATING RESULTS:		Team		1			
58	Productivity		15	15	15	15	NA	NA
59	Recruits/redundancies		1	1	1	1	NA	NA
60	Leavers		1	1	1	1	NA	NA
61	Employees (end qtr)	7	7	7	7	7	NA	NA
62	Actual production		50	60	60	55	NA	NA
63	Overtime production		0	0	0	0	NA	NA
64	Overtime pay £		0	0	0	0	NA	NA
65	Customer orders		27	78	72	28	50	100
66	(A=actual, E=estimated)		A	A	A	A	E	E
67	Sales		27	78	72	28	NA	NA
68								
69	Stock levels and values at end of each quarter:							
70	Raw material stock	50	60	60	60	55	NA	NA
71	Raw material cost £	40	40.00	40.00	41.00	41.00	43.00	43.00
72	Finished goods stock	10	33	15	3	30	NA	NA
73	Finished goods cost £	450	558	514	495	530	NA	NA
74	Total stock value £	6500	20825	10114	3945	18155	NA	NA

Figure A1.5 The operating results screen

Overtime pay (£) (row 64): the total overtime pay for all staff due to overtime working (if any).

Customer orders (row 65): the total orders you receive from customers who want to buy your products in the quarter.

The row underneath (row 66) shows either an A for an actual order calculated by the simulation, or E for an estimate made by the user when you enter any number in row 54 on the decisions screen.

Sales (row 67): the units you sold during the quarter.

Note that for the next four rows, column B shows the stock levels and values at the end of 'quarter 0', i.e. at the start of quarter one.

Raw material stock (row 70): the amount of raw materials you have in stock at the end of each quarter, which can be used in the future.

Raw material cost (£) (row 71): the unit cost of raw materials each quarter.

Finished goods stock (row 72): the amount of finished goods left in stock at the end of the quarter, which can be sold in future quarters.

Finished goods cost (£) (row 73): the average cost of producing one unit of finished goods in the quarter, copied from row 157.

Total stock value (£) (row 74): the total value of stocks at the end of the quarter (finished goods plus raw materials).

		A	B	C	D	E	F	G	H
1	SMF.WK1	Quarter	0	1	2	3	4	5	6
2				Press F9 for trial run, Alt M for menu					
75	PROFIT AND LOSS:			Team		1			
76									
77	Revenue			18900	54600	50400	19600	NA	NA
78	Cost of goods			15075	40111	35629	14840	NA	NA
79	Gross profit			3825	14489	14771	4760	NA	NA
80									
81	Operating expenses			6390	10060	9840	6960	NA	NA
82	Operating profit			−2565	4429	4931	−2200	NA	NA
83									
84	Loan interest			−625	−625	−625	−625	−425	−425
85	C/A interest			−766	−1844	−1997	−1505	NA	NA
86	Net profit			−3956	1960	2309	−4330	NA	NA
87									
88	Tax due						0		
89									
90	RETAINED PROFIT			−3956	1960	2309	−4330	NA	NA
91									
92									

Figure A1.6   The profit and loss screen

Profit and loss (see Figure A1.6)

Revenue (row 77): the total income for the quarter, derived from the number of sales multiplied by your selling price.

Cost of goods (row 78): defined as the total value of stock at the start of the quarter, plus the cost of materials purchased, basic salaries and overtime, salary related overheads, depreciation of plant and equipment, less the total value of stock at the end of the quarter.

Gross profit (row 79): revenue less cost of goods.

Operating expenses (row 81): fixed overheads plus the costs of advertising, recruitment, redundancy and distribution.

Operating profit (row 82): gross profit less operating expenses. This reflects the profit being made from the trading activities of the business, and excludes any interest earned or paid or tax paid.

Loan interest (row 84): interest paid on your loan.

Current account interest (row 85): interest earned or paid on your current account.

Net profit (row 86): operating profit plus or minus all interest charges. Any losses are carried forward and are offset against profits in future years. For example, the cumulative losses in year one were:

- − £3956 in quarter one
- + £1960 in quarter two
- + £2309 in quarter three, and
- − £4330 in quarter four

This amounts to a loss of £4017 for the first year as a whole. You will need to make a profit of more than this in the second year for any tax to be due.

Tax due (row 88): any tax due, calculated at the prevailing rate (30 per cent currently). Tax is only due in the last quarter of each year, i.e. quarters four, eight and twelve.

Retained profit (row 90): net profit less tax due (if any). This represents the profit earned which may be retained in the business.

Balance sheet (see Figure A1.7)

Plant and equipment (row 94): the value of your production plant and equipment, which depreciates over a period of five years currently. It does not wear out, however, and will be fully effective for the duration of the simulation.

Land and buildings (row 95): the value of the premises and land they are built on. These do not depreciate (or appreciate).

Current assets: cash (row 96): the money not currently required, which you have invested in the bank at the end of each quarter.

Current assets: debtors (row 97): money owed to you by customers who have not yet paid you. They will all pay in due course (half in the quarter following sales, and half the quarter after that).

	A	B	C	D	E	F	G	H
1	SMF.WK1	Quarter	0	1	2	3	4	5	6
2				Press F9 for trial run, Alt M for menu					
93	BALANCE SHEET:			Team	1			
94	Plant & equipment			11400	10800	10200	9600	9000	8400
95	Land & buildings			75000	75000	75000	75000	75000	75000
96	Current assets: cash			0	0	0	0	NA	NA
97	debtors			18900	64050	77700	44800	NA	NA
98	stocks			20825	10114	3945	18155	NA	NA
99									
100	Current liabs: overdraft			22681	54560	59072	44522	NA	NA
101	creditors			2400	2400	2460	2050	NA	NA
102	tax due						0		
103									
104	NET ASSETS			101044	103004	105313	100983	NA	NA
105									
106	Share capital			80000	80000	80000	80000	80000	80000
107	Cum retained profit			–3956	–1996	313	–4017	NA	NA
108	Loans			25000	25000	25000	25000	17000	17000
109	CAPITAL EMPLOYED			101044	103004	105313	100983	NA	NA
110				0	0	0	0	NA	NA

Figure A1.7   *The balance sheet screen*

Current assets: stocks (row 98): the total value of stocks (raw materials and finished goods) at the end of each quarter.

Current liabilities: overdraft (row 100): the amount you are overdrawn at the bank at the end of each quarter.

Current liabilities: creditors (row 101): money you owe to raw material suppliers. You will have to pay this the following quarter.

Current liabilities: tax due (row 102): if any, to be paid in the next quarter.

Net assets (row 104): the total value of the company, defined as the value of plant and equipment, land and buildings, plus all current assets, less all current liabilities.

Share capital (row 106): the amount of money you as owner invested in the company when you started it up.

Cumulative retained profits (row 107): the sum of all retained profits (less losses, if any) up to date.

The total of the share capital and the cumulative retained profits is defined as the owner's equity, which is the amount of the business owned, as opposed to supported by a loan.

Loans (row 108): the size of any loan outstanding.

Capital employed (row 109): this is the total amount of money invested in the firm, defined by the share capital plus cumulative retained profits and loans. It is by definition always equal to the net assets of the company.

Row 110 contains a check sum for each quarter. If the figures shown here are not zero, there is a rounding error in the spreadsheet since the capital employed is not equal to the net assets.

Sources of cash (see Figure A1.8)

Opening cash/overdraft (row 113): the cash or overdraft at the start of each quarter. It is equal to the closing cash balance or overdraft (see row 146 below) at the end of the previous quarter.

Opening debtors (row 115): the total amount of money outstanding and owed to you as debtors at the start of the quarter.

Revenue (row 117): money from sales during the quarter.

Closing debtors (row 119): the total amount of money outstanding and owed to you by customers at the end of the quarter.

In Quarter One, closing debtors are defined as the revenue earned in Quarter One. In Quarter Two, closing debtors are defined as:

opening debtors in Quarter Two,
plus revenue earned in Quarter Two,
less half of the revenue earned in Quarter One.

In other words, no Quarter Two customers pay you in Quarter Two, and only half of Quarter One customers do so.

	A	B	C	D	E	F	G	H
1	SMF.WK1	Quarter	0	1	2	3	4	5	6
2				Press F9 for trial run, Alt M for menu				
111	SOURCES OF CASH:			Team		1		
112								
113	Opening cash/o-d			−21000	−22681	−54560	−59072	−44522	NA
114								
115	Opening debtors			9500	18900	64050	77700	44800	NA
116								
117	Revenue			18900	54600	50400	19600	NA	NA
118								
119	Closing debtors			18900	64050	77700	44800	NA	NA
120								
121	Net recd from debtors			9500	9450	36750	52500	NA	NA
122								
123	New loans			25000	0	0	0	0	0
124								
125	Total cash available			13500	−13231	−17810	−6572	NA	NA
126								
127								
128								

Figure A1.8 *The sources of cash screen*

In Quarter Three and beyond, closing debtors are defined thus:

> opening debtors in the quarter,
> plus revenue earned in the quarter,
> less half of the revenue earned in the preceding two quarters.

Net received from debtors (row 121): the total amount of cash paid to you by debtors during the quarter, defined as the opening debtors, plus revenue, less closing debtors.

Note: due to the use of credit cards and the arrangements you have made with your trade customers, you receive half the cash from sales in the quarter following the sale, and the other half the quarter after that.

New loans (row 123): the money received in the form of loans during any quarter. You have a loan of £25 000 which was granted in quarter one, part of which must be repaid in quarters five and nine. Any change in these arrangements must be agreed with the administrator.

Total cash available (row 125): this is the only cash available in the quarter, and is the sum of net cash received from debtors and new loans plus the initial cash (or less initial overdraft).

Cash uses and balance (see Figure A1.9)

Opening creditors (row 130): the money owed by your company to suppliers of raw materials at the start of the quarter.

Material costs (row 131): the cost of materials bought during the quarter.

	A	B	C	D	E	F	G	H
1 SMF.WK1	Quarter	0	1	2	3	4	5	6
2			Press F9 for trial run, Alt M for menu					
129 CASH USES & BALANCE:			Team		1			
130 Opening creditors			2000	2400	2400	2460	2050	NA
131 Material costs			2400	2400	2460	2050	NA	NA
132 Closing creditors			2400	2400	2460	2050	NA	NA
133 Net paid to creditors			2000	2400	2400	2460	NA	NA
134 Salaries and overtime			24000	24000	24000	24000	NA	NA
135 Recruitment/redundancy			1000	1000	1000	1000	NA	NA
136 Tax paid			0	0	0	0	0	0
137 Advertising			500	600	800	1000	NA	NA
138 Distribution costs			1890	5460	5040	1960	NA	NA
139 Overheads			5400	5400	5400	5400	NA	NA
140 Loan repaid			0	0	0	0	8000	0
141 Loan interest			625	625	625	625	425	425
142								
143 Total cash out			35415	39485	39265	36445	NA	NA
144 Balance			−21915	−52716	−57075	−43017	NA	NA
145 Current a/c interest			−766	−1844	−1997	−1505	NA	NA
146 Closing cash balance			−22681	−54560	−59072	−44522	NA	NA

Figure A1.9 The cash uses and balance screen

Closing creditors (row 132): the money owed by the company to raw material suppliers at the end of the quarter. This is the same as the material costs for the quarter.

Net paid to creditors (row 133): the nett amount of cash the company paid to creditors during the quarter. Your creditors are the suppliers of raw materials, and you have to pay these after one quarter, more quickly than you are paid by your customers. Other expenses such as advertising and salaries are paid immediately. The net payment is defined as the opening creditors, plus materials costs, less closing creditors.

Salaries and overtime (row 134): total salaries including overtime payments, if any, based on the number of employees you had at the end of the previous quarter (row 61) plus recruits this quarter (row 59). Any redundancies you have this quarter will not reduce your salary bill in the current quarter, only in the next quarter, due to the one-quarter notice you give to employees.

Recruitment/redundancy cost (row 135): the cost of recruiting or making staff redundant.

Tax paid (row 136): the amount of tax paid during the quarter. Tax is paid in the first quarter of the following year (i.e. quarter five for the first year and quarter nine for the second year).

Advertising (row 137): the amount of money you decided to spend on advertising.

Distribution costs (row 138): the amount of money the company spends on delivering goods to customers, equivalent to 10 per cent of revenue.

Overheads (row 139): fixed overheads plus salary-related overheads. The fixed overheads are, as the name implies, independent of the volume of business and therefore independent of any of your decisions. They represent rent, council charges, insurance and the cost of water, gas or electricity. Salary-related overheads include the cost of national insurance, training, etc. and for simplicity are set at 10 per cent of salaries.

Loan repaid (row 140): the cash involved in repaying a loan, if any.

Loan interest (row 141): the interest charges associated with any outstanding loan, calculated on the basis of the loan outstanding at the end of the current quarter.

Total cash out (row 143): the sum of all items above from row 133 to row 141.

Balance (row 144): total cash available (from sources of cash screen), less total cash out (row 143).

Current account interest (row 145): the interest on the balance at the prevailing current account interest rate. This is calculated on the balance at the end of each quarter, as shown in row 144.

Closing Cash Balance (row 146): the final balance at the end of each quarter, defined as the balance in row 144 plus or minus current account interest in row 145.

Key ratios (see Figure A1.10)

Liquidity (row 149): current assets (cash plus debtors plus stocks) divided by current liabilities (overdraft, creditors and tax due). This ratio is an indication of the extent to which you are able to pay your bills in the short term. Traditionally the ratio should be above two. If by any chance current liabilities are zero, the liquidity ratio will be set to zero to avoid division by zero, which would result in an error.

Profit/sales (% pa) (row 150): operating profit as a percentage of revenue.

Gearing (row 151): loan and overdraft (if any), as a proportion of share capital plus cumulative retained profit. This shows the proportion of the business which is borrowed.

Return on equity (% pa) (row 153): profit before tax as a percentage of equity (share capital plus cumulative retained profit). This shows the annual before-tax return the owners are achieving on their investment.

ROCE (% pa) (row 154) (Return on Capital Employed): this is the annual operating profit as a percentage of capital employed plus overdraft (if any). This ratio shows what return the business is earning on all its assets.

Advertising/sales per cent (row 156): advertising as a percentage of revenue.

	A	B	C	D	E	F	G	H
1 SMF.WK1	Quarter	0	1	2	3	4	5	6
2			Press F9 for trial run, Alt M for menu					
147 KEY RATIOS:			Team		1			
148								
149 Liquidity			1.6	1.3	1.3	1.4	NA	NA
150 Profit/sales % pa			−13.6	8.1	9.8	−11.2	NA	NA
151 Gearing			0.63	1.02	1.05	0.91	NA	NA
152								
153 Return on equity % pa			−20.8	10.0	11.5	−22.8	NA	NA
154 ROCE % pa			−8.3	11.2	12.0	−6.0	NA	NA
155								
156 Advertising/sales %			2.6	1.1	1.6	5.1	NA	NA
157 Unit cost £			558	514	495	530	NA	NA
158 Profit £ per employee			−565	280	330	−619	NA	NA
159								
160 Staff turnover %			14.3	14.3	14.3	14.3	NA	NA
161 Productivity			15	15	15	15	NA	NA
162 Customer service %			100	100	100	100	NA	NA
163								
164								

Figure A1.10   *The key ratios screen*

Unit cost (£) (row 157): defined as the total stock value at the start of the quarter, plus total pay including overtime, cost of materials purchased, salary-related overheads and depreciation, less the raw material stock value at the end of the quarter, all divided by the finished goods stock at the start of the quarter plus the amount produced in the quarter. This will fluctuate from quarter to quarter as stocks vary.

Profit £ per employee (row 158): net profit per employee at the end of the previous quarter.

Staff turnover (% per quarter) (row 160): leavers during the quarter as a percentage of the employees at the end of the previous quarter. Due to the low employee numbers and the fact that there may be no leavers at all in some quarters, this figure will fluctuate. For example, a single employee leaving among a staff of seven would give a turnover of 14.3 per cent in a quarter.

Productivity (row 161): the maximum number of units per quarter that one employee can manufacture in normal working hours.

Customer service (%) (row 162): sales as a percentage of orders in the quarter.

Using the simulation

Figure A1.11 shows in simplified terms how the various parts of the spreadsheet are interrelated. Note that in most simulations the user is only able to enter decisions and receive results, and is not able to see the way those results are calculated. Because of the transparent nature of spreadsheets, all the calculations are present as well as decision input and display of results and it would be possible to 'cheat' in a number of ways. For example, the basic economic data underlying the simulation, costs, inflation rates, market demands and all the formulae determining the product orders are all part of the same spreadsheet and it would be possible for the user to study these. To avoid casual inspection, the base data and market and employee calculations are all arranged at the bottom of the spreadsheet.

If you wish to use the simulation properly, do not study the base data or market/employee screens too closely (the contents should be hidden beyond quarter five to avoid casual inspection). The economic data for the forthcoming quarter will be revealed on the 'Economic Data' screen one quarter at a time after the current quarter has been run. Also the many NA entries appearing in the results will disappear after genuine decisions are made. The decisions for the quarter you have just completed should be protected using a macro, preventing rerunning of the same quarter more than once.

Having become familiar with the layout of the simulation, proceed as follows for quarter five.

1 Study the economic data which is always visible from the first quarter up to the quarter you are about to play. Also look at the decisions

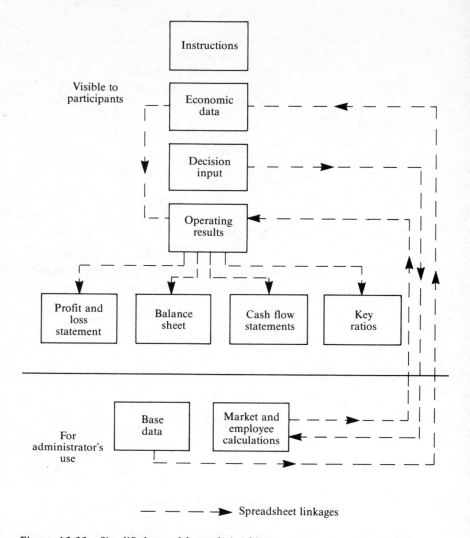

Figure A1.11 *Simplified spreadsheet relationships*

that have been made during the first four quarters, and the financial and operating results that have been achieved.

2 Note the values of the resources that will limit your actions in the next quarter. For example, in quarter five the operating results' screen shows:

raw material stock (row 70), 55 at the end of quarter four,
finished goods stock (row 72), 30 at the end of quarter four,
productivity (row 58), 15 in quarter four, and
employees at the end of the quarter (row 61), 7 at the end of quarter four.

Therefore, during quarter five, 30 units of furniture are available for sale even if no more are produced in the quarter. If no materials were bought in quarter five then the 55 units of raw material would still be available for use in production in quarter six, less those used for production in quarter five. The maximum production possible in quarter five can be estimated by assuming the productivity in quarter five will be the same as in quarter four (i.e. 15), and multiplying this by the number of employees (7) and by 1.25 to allow for overtime. This gives a maximum production of 131. Unfortunately only 55 units of raw material are available at the end of quarter four, and this will therefore act as the effective production limit.

The upper limit on sales is therefore the 55 that can be produced in quarter five, plus the 30 already in stock, giving a total of 85.

Also keep a close eye on the overdraft (row 100), and try to keep this less than £100 000. Any increase above this level should be agreed with the simulation administrator.

3 Make tentative decisions and enter them on the decision screen for quarter five. Note that the screen should be unprotected from quarter five onwards. It is useful to remind yourself of your overall objectives, which are to become better known by raising the general level of awareness among your potential clients, to produce reasonably priced goods in the desired quantities, to be a good employer and to be profitable.
4 Bearing in mind the decisions you have just made, the previous customer demand and the seasonal factor (20 per cent in quarter five, i.e. double the seasonal factor in quarter four, when customer orders were 28), enter an estimate of the orders you expect to receive in row 54. Remember that this should be as accurate as possible.

Press Calc to see the results of these decisions. Then use PgUp and PgDn to study the operating and financial results fully. Print out some sections of the simulation for further study if you wish, as explained in step 5. The following instructions describe a number of macros which should be developed by the user.

5 Hold down Alt and press M. A menu will appear at the top of the screen and various subsidiary menus could be developed as shown in Figure A1.12.

With the menu in view, use the left or right arrow keys (*not* the initial letter of the option you require, as there is sometimes more than one entry for the same letter).

Go To to move around the screen.
Run to run the simulation (do not do this until you are happy about your decisions; once you have run a quarter you cannot rerun it). *Note*: before running the simulation you must set the estimated orders in the current quarter (row 54) to zero or the simulation will not function properly.
Print to print various results.
Save to save the current version of the spreadsheet, so you can continue on another occasion if desired. After choosing this option

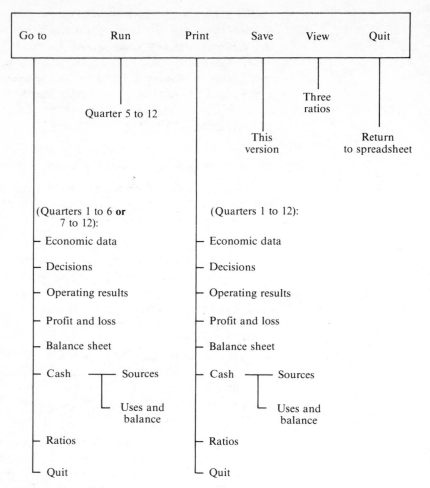

Figure A1.12   SMF menus

the top of the screen will show the current file name. If you wish to change the name, press Esc, type the new name and press Enter. If you wish to use the same name press Enter when the existing file name appears. You will be prompted to say whether you wish to cancel the request to save the file, replace the current version or produce a backup copy.

View graphs could show three financial ratios, the liquidity ratio (row 149), profit/sales (row 150) and ROCE (row 154). If the graph is not in colour and you have a colour monitor, escape from the menu and press/GOC (graph options colour).

Quit to remove the menu and return to the spreadsheet.

Each option could provide further options as follows. In each case one of two options can be chosen, either for Quarters One to Six or for Quarters Seven to Twelve.

Go To Economic data (see Figure A1.3)
         Decisions (see Figure A1.4)

Operating results (see Figure A1.5)
Profit and loss (see Figure A1.6)
Balance sheet (see Figure A1.7)
Sources of cash (see Figure A1.8)
Cash uses and balance (see Figure A1.9)
Key ratios (see Figure A1.10)
Quit to return to main menu

Print   Economic data ⎫   prints all twelve quarters, but only
                        shows quarter one up to the quarter in
          Decisions ⎭   which you are about to make decisions
          Operating results   prints results
                        from quarter
          Profit and loss   one to
                        the last
          Balance sheet   quarter
                        for which
          Sources and uses of   decisions
          cash   have been
          Ratios   made.

6 Repeat steps 3 to 5 as often as you like, but remember you are only estimating orders (you will see an E in row 66 to remind you about this). When you are ready to proceed with quarter five move on to step 7.

7 Set the estimated orders in the current quarter (row 54) to zero before running the simulation. Thus for quarter five set the cell G54 to zero. Press Alt M to see the menu. Highlight Run and choose the appropriate quarter. After a second or two the results will be computed. Use the menu to study the results carefully, and print them out if required. Return to step 1 for the next quarter.

Administrator's guide

The simulation is intended for sixth form or higher education use, or for anyone wanting an introduction to some of the problems involved in running a small business, particularly the financial aspects. Users will need a basic understanding of business and financial terminology.

Participants may continue to run the simulation right through to quarter twelve at one time, or they may pause after a few quarters and continue later. If pausing it is essential that they save the current state of the simulation, using a different file name. The spreadsheet could occupy about 70kb of disc space, so several versions may be held on the same disc.

Brief   The *Participant's Guide* answers most questions and this may be supplemented with other material as required. Participants wishing to gain a firm grasp of how cash flow, profit and loss and balance sheets are composed should be given a set of printed pro formas as shown in Figures A1.13, A1.14 and A1.15. Figure A1.13 shows the decisions taken for the first four quarters and the operating results that were achieved. Figures A1.14 and A1.15 show the accounts for the first three quarters. These include all the information necessary to work out the accounts for Quarter Four.

Remember that the spreadsheet can only be used by one person or group at a time. If you wish a number of individuals or groups to take part in the simulation simultaneously, make several copies of the spreadsheet and give one copy to each individual or group. Participants may then be divided into groups of up to four, depending on the number of computers available.

Timetable An approximate timetable for running SMF is as follows:

- reading the *Participant's Guide* and oral briefing: 40–60 minutes
- completion of accounts for quarter four (optional): 40–60 minutes
- analysis and decisions for quarter five, printing results: up to 40 minutes
- quarters six to eight: 20–30 minutes per quarter
- set objectives for quarters nine to twelve (optional): 20–30 minutes
- analysis and decisions for quarters nine to twelve, printing results: 20 minutes each

The end of the simulation could usefully be followed by an interval to absorb results, followed by debrief lasting 30 to 40 minutes, depending on the number of teams. The simulation could therefore ideally be run over a few days, occupying between four and seven hours as required.

		Quarters			
Decisions:		1	2	3	4
Planned production (units)		50	60	60	55
Materials bought (units)		60	60	60	50
Price (£)		700	700	700	700
Advertising (£)		500	600	800	1000
Employees (+ or −)		1	1	1	1
Basic pay (£)		3000	3000	3000	3000
Operating results:					
Recruits/redundancies		1	1	1	1
Leavers		1	1	1	1
Employees (end qtr)	7	7	7	7	7
Actual production		50	60	60	55
Overtime production		0	0	0	0
Overtime pay (£)		0	0	0	0
Customer orders		27	78	72	28
Sales		27	78	72	28
Stock levels and values at end of each quarter:					
Raw material stock	50	60	60	60	55
Raw material cost (£)	40	40.00	40.00	41.00	41.00
Finished goods stock	10	33	15	3	30
Finished goods cost (£)	450	558	514	495	530
Total stock value (£)	6500	20 825	10 114	3945	18 155

Figure A1.13 Decisions and operating results pro forma

Sources of cash:	Quarters			
	1	2	3	4
Opening cash/o-d	−21 000	−22 681	−54 560	
Opening debtors	9500	18 900	64 050	
Revenue	18 900	54 600	50 400	
Nett rec'd from debtors	9500	9450	36 750	
New loans	25 000	0	0	
Total cash available	13 500	−13 231	−17 810	
Cash uses and balance:				
Opening creditors	2000	2400	2400	
Material costs	2400	2400	2460	
Closing creditors	2400	2400	2460	
Net paid to creditors	2000	2400	2400	
Salaries and overtime	24 000	24 000	24 000	
Recruitment/redundancy	1000	1000	1000	
Tax paid	0	0	0	
Advertising	500	600	800	
Distribution costs	1890	5460	5040	
Overheads	5400	5400	5400	
Loan repaid	0	0	0	
Loan interest	625	625	625	
Total cash out	35 415	39 485	39 265	
Balance	−21 915	−52 716	−57 075	
C/A interest	−766	−1844	−1997	
Closing cash balance	−22 681	−54 560	−59 072	

Figure A1.14   *Cash flow pro forma*

Debrief   This could include general comments from the administrator, a statement of each team's objectives, a comparison of results against objectives for each team and a discussion of the differences, and an assessment of the relative performance of each team, using a number of criteria such as:

- relationships with administrator in the role of banker (including their repayment of loan, final overdraft, etc.)
- how good an employer was each team? (number of employees, redundancies, pay levels, productivity, staff turnover from key ratios screen)
- how well did they treat customers? (market share, reputation for price and for service, actual price and customer satisfaction from key ratios screen)
- financial performance (for example, information shown on the key ratios screen)

Loading the simulation   Load Lotus 123, place the disc containing the simulation file and retrieve the file using:

/FR
Point to SMF.WK1 (or whatever file name has been used to save the spreadsheet) and press Enter

	Quarters			
Profit and loss:	1	2	3	4
Revenue	18 900	54 600	50 400	
Cost of goods	15 075	40 111	35 629	
Gross profit	3825	14 489	14 771	
Operating expenses	6390	10 060	9840	
Operating profit	−2565	4429	4931	
Loan interest	−625	−625	−625	
C/A interest	−766	−1844	−1997	
Net profit	−3956	1960	2309	
Tax due				
Retained profit	−3956	1960	2309	
Balance sheet:				
Plant and equipment	11 400	10 800	10 200	
Land and buildings	75 000	75 000	75 000	
Current assets: cash	0	0	0	
debtors	18 900	64 050	77 700	
stocks	20 825	10 114	3945	
Current liabilities: overdraft	22 681	54 560	59 072	
creditors	2400	2400	2460	
tax due				
Net assets	101 044	103 004	105 313	
Share capital	80 000	80 000	80 000	
Cumulative retained profit	−3956	−1996	313	
Loans	25 000	25 000	25 000	
Capital employed	101 044	103 004	105 313	
Key ratios:				
Liquidity	1.6	1.3	1.3	
Profit/sales % pa	−13.6	8.1	9.8	
Gearing	0.63	1.02	1.05	
Return on equity % pa	−20.8	10.0	11.5	
ROCE % pa	−8.3	11.2	12.0	

Figure A1.15   Profit and loss, balance sheet and key ratios pro forma

Refer to the screen layout in Figure A1.1 to see how the whole spreadsheet is arranged and the relationships diagram shown in Figure A1.11 for the relationships between the various parts. Participants should enter their team number in cell E3.

The first screen gives a reminder of what the simulation is and how to use it. Browse around the spreadsheet using PgUp, PgDn or Ctrl→ and Ctrl←. Most figures in the accounts will show NA beyond quarter four. This is normal, and the correct figures will show for each quarter when decisions have been made for the quarter.

Macros   For simplicity of operation, the spreadsheet can be driven by a number of fairly straightforward macros. These allow the user to move around the spreadsheet easily, print out results and, most important, to run the simulation one quarter at a time. If it were not for the way the spreadsheet is protected, it would be easily possible for the casual user to use it like any other spreadsheet, and simply 're-invent the past' by rerunning previous quarters as often as desired (this is, however, still possible for the determined user). When the spreadsheet is run using the macro, the next quarter's economic data are revealed and the previous decisions and results are protected. Access the menu by holding down Alt and pressing M.

The macros can be held in columns well away from the screens used by participants.

Administrator's screens   To change any of the data on the administrator's screens (either the base data screen or the market/employee calculations screen), make the required cells visible if necessary, unprotect them, make the required changes and protect and hide the cells afterwards.

Use the command /RFR and specify the desired range to make any cells visible. Then use the command /RU to unprotect the required range. Reverse the process when you have finished.

Base data   Use PgDn until you see the base data screen shown in Figure A1.16 This is not accessible using the menu, although participants will be able to see the screen by using PgDn and PgUp. Access the screen containing data for quarters seven to twelve using Ctrl→.

	A	B	C	D	E	F	G	H
1	SMF.WK1	Quarter	0	1	2	3	4	5	6
2				Press F9 for trial run, Alt M for menu					
165	BASE DATA:			For administrator's use only!					
166									
167	Loan+/repayment−			25 000	0	0	0	−8000	0
168	Loan interest % pa			10					
169	O/draft interest % pa			14.00	14.00	14.00	14.00	14.00	14.00
170	Current a/c interest % pa			7.00	7.00	7.00	7.00	7.00	7.00
171									
172	Inflation index			100	102	103	105	107	109
173									
174	Tax rate % pa			30.00					
175									
176	Raw material cost £		40	40.00	40.00	41.00	41.00	43.00	43.00
177									
178	Overheads: £ fixed			3000	3000	3000	3000	3200	3200
179	% salaries			10					
180									
181	Lifetime of plant and equipment			5 yrs. Quarterly deprecn.					600
182									

Figure A1.16   The base data screen

Row 167 shows the loan +/repayment−. You will see that currently a loan of £25 000 was granted in quarter one, (cell C167), and repayments are as follows:

−£8000 in quarter five (cell G167), and
−£8000 in quarter nine (cell K167).

Note the negative signs indicating repayments. The loan of £25 000 in cell C167 was entered as a positive number. Use the same convention if you wish to amend row 167.

Cell C168 shows the loan interest (% pa). Note that this interest rate applies to all loans granted at any time throughout the twelve quarters.

Rows 169 and 170 contain the current account overdraft interest rate and current account interest rate (earned on balances) respectively. These should differ by a few percentage points to reflect reality.

Row 172 is the inflation index. Note that the index for quarter one is set at 100 for simplicity. Inflation occurring subsequently can therefore be related back to this quarter. As an example, quarter five shows that the inflation index will be 107. This represents a 7 per cent increase over quarter one, i.e. in the first year, but only a 7/105 or a 1.9 per cent increase over quarter four.

Inflation affects customers' perceptions of price and employees perceptions of pay. Participants should therefore endeavour if possible to keep both prices and pay in line with inflation. Also the effect of advertising will reduce unless advertising expenditure is kept abreast of inflation.

Cell C174 contains the tax rate, currently set at 30 per cent.

Row 176 contains the raw material unit costs, which are specified separately from inflation.

Row 178 shows fixed overheads, also specified separately from inflation. These are intended to reflect the cost of rents and council charges, insurance, heating and lighting, etc.

Cell C179 is the percentage of salaries used to calculate certain overhead charges which depend on the number of staff employed and their pay levels. These would represent, for example, national insurance and office expenses.

Cell D181 is the lifetime of plant and equipment in years, used as the basis of plant and equipment depreciation. The straight-line method is used, so since the value of plant and equipment at the start of Quarter One was £12 000 and the lifetime is five years, depreciation per quarter is calculated thus:

initial plant value/(plant life × 4)
= £12 000/(5 × 4) = £600

This result is shown in cell H181.

	A	B	C	D	E	F	G	H
1 SMF.WK1	Quarter	0	1	2	3	4	5	6
2			Press F9 for trial run, Alt M for menu					
183 MARKET/EMPLOYEE CALCULATIONS:			For administrator's use only!					
184								
185 Approx seasonal effect			20%	40%	30%	10%	20%	40%
186								
187 Potential market size			800	1600	1200	400		
188 Smoothed advertising			16.2	20.2	24.0	27.5	NA	NA
189								
190 Awareness %			18.5	21.5	24.3	26.7	NA	NA
191								
192 Reputation for service			75	88	94	97	98	NA
193 Price reputation			25	26	27	28	NA	NA
194								
195 Market share %			3.5	4.9	6.0	7.1	NA	NA
196 Orders			27	78	72	28	NA	NA
197								
198 Pay ratio			1.00	0.98	0.97	0.95	NA	NA
199 Productivity			15	15	15	15	NA	NA
200 Leavers			1	1	1	1	NA	NA

Figure A1.17 *The market/employee calculations screen*

Market/employee calculations

Now PgDn once more to inspect the market/employee calculations screen as shown in Figure A1.17. Once again these show NA beyond Quarter Four until genuine decisions are entered.

Row 185 shows the approximate seasonal effect in each quarter. This shows that the demand experienced in the first quarter of each year will be approximately 20 per cent of the annual total, and demand in the second quarter will be 40 per cent, etc. This row acts as a reminder to the administrator, but is not used in any formulae.

Row 187 shows the potential market size which should be roughly in proportion to the seasonal factors. The figures are hidden beyond Quarter Four, but may be seen by placing the cursor over the required cell.

Row 188 contains the smoothed advertising, calculated thus:

> current value of smoothed advertising =
> 0.5 × previous value of smoothed advertising
> + 0.5 × square root of (current advertising £ × quarter one inflation index/current inflation index)

The smoothing of advertising has the following effect. Suppose that advertising expenditure has been increased exactly in line with inflation from Quarters One to Six. In Quarter Six the advertising effect is calculated from all previous values, but the effects of previous quarters' advertising diminish by 50 per cent each quarter as follows:

quarter	6	5	4	3	previous quarters
advertising effect	0.5	0.25	0.125	0.0625	0.0625

Row 190 shows the customer awareness, calculated thus:

> awareness = 95 − 90 × (0.99 raised to the power of smoothed advertising)
> where smoothed advertising is defined as above

The customer awareness is defined to be in the range 5 to 95 per cent and is shown in Figure A1.18.

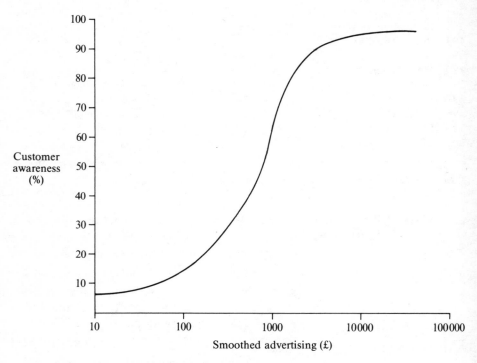

Figure A1.18   *Customer awareness*

Row 192 contains the calculations for reputation for service, as shown in Figure 6.5. However, the actual reputation for service is smoothed in a similar manner to the advertising, as follows:

> reputation for service = previous quarter's reputation for service × 0.5
> + 0.5 × previous quarter's customer service level (from row 162)

This formula gives the reputation in the range 0 to 100 per cent. In row 162 previous orders are defined as the maximum of rows 54 and 65, i.e. the maximum of estimated orders and actual orders. This means that when participants are using the 'what if?' planning facility by entering an estimated orders figure in row 54, the entry in row 54 will be assumed in row 192. When the estimated figure is set to zero the actual demand calculated by the simulation and shown in row 65 will be used in rows 162 and 192. Note that the reputation for service starts with an arbitrary 75 per cent in cell C192.

Row 193 shows the price reputation defined by:

25 × (current price/quarter 1 price × quarter 1 inflation index/ current inflation index)$^{-2}$

This formula is subject to a lower limit of 10 per cent and an upper limit of 100 per cent. Figure A1.19 shows the results graphically.

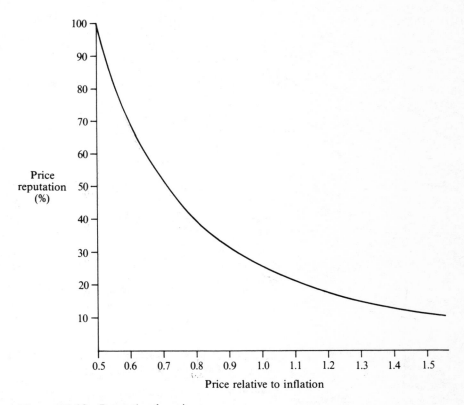

Figure A1.19   *Reputation for price*

Figure A1.20 shows the combined reputation for both price and service.

Row 195 of the market/employee calculations screen shows the market share which is defined as:

awareness (row 190)
× reputation for service (row 192)
× reputation for price (row 193) / 10 000

This gives a market share in the range 0 to 95 per cent.

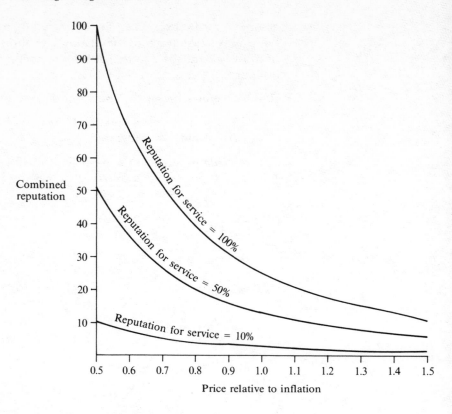

Figure A1.20   Combined reputation for price and service

Row 196 contains the orders calculation, as follows:

> orders = potential market size (row 187)
> $\qquad\qquad$ × market share (row 195) / 100

Row 198 is the pay ratio, defined as:

> pay in current quarter/pay in quarter 1 (row 51)
> $\qquad$ × inflation index in quarter 1/current inflation index (row 172)

Row 199 is the productivity, defined as:

> 5 + 10 × pay ratio raised to the power of 0.6

The pay ratio is defined above and in this formula the pay ratio is limited to a range of 0.5 to 1.5. Figure A1.21 shows the employee productivity.

Row 200 shows the leavers calculated from the employee turnover, defined as:

> $(2 + 10 \times (\text{pay ratio})^{-2})/100$

where the pay ratio is defined as above, but again limited to the 0.5 to 1.5 range. This formula gives an employee turnover in the range 6 to 42 per cent per quarter, but since actual leavers must obviously be

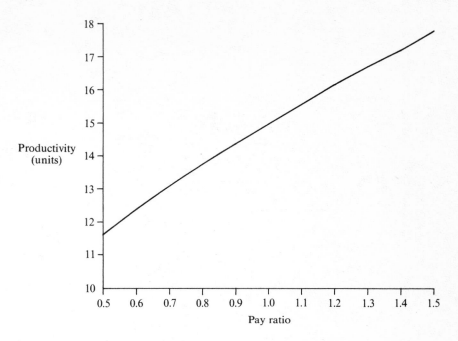

Figure A1.21 Productivity

rounded to the nearest whole number, actual turnover (shown on row 160 of the key ratios screen Figure A1.10), may differ from this. Figure A1.22 shows the employee turnover.

Notes on the results

These notes provide additional information which will help the administrator understand the design and use of the spreadsheet.

Capital allowances

For simplicity, tax is calculated directly as 30 per cent of the net profit shown on the profit and loss account. This net profit figure has been calculated by deducting depreciation of plant and equipment on a 'straight line' basis, as explained in the *Participant's Guide*. The initial value of plant and equipment was £12 000, so if this has a five-year life the annual depreciation will be £2400, equivalent to £600 per quarter. To comply strictly with UK tax law (and with similar legislation in many other countries), the depreciation charge should be substituted with a legally prescribed 'capital allowance'. This is currently calculated at 25 per cent per annum of the reducing balance, as follows:

> 25 per cent of £12 000 or £3000 in year one,
> 25 per cent of the remainder (£12 000 less £3000 or £9000), or £2250 in year two, and
> 25 per cent of the remainder (£9000 less £2250 or £6750), or £1688 in year three.

If an understanding of business taxation is of concern to participants then the administrator may wish to draw their attention to this simplification.

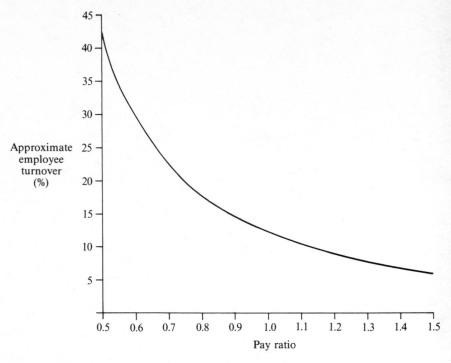

Figure A1.22   Employee turnover

Operating results (see Figure A1.5)

Leavers (row 60) are copied from row 200.

Employees (row 61)

> = employees at the end of the previous quarter (row 61)
> + actual recruits or redundancies (row 59)
> − leavers (row 60)

Actual production (row 62) is the minimum of A, B and C, where:

A = maximum of planned production (row 41), and customer orders less existing stock (row 65 less row 72),

B = employees at the start of the quarter (row 61) × productivity (row 199) × 1.25 (to allow for maximum overtime), and

C = material stock at the end of the previous quarter (row 70).

This shows that, as in reality, it is possible to increase actual production above planned levels if demand warrants it, subject to constraints imposed by raw material stock, employee numbers and productivity.

Overtime production (row 63) is calculated as follows:

> if actual production exceeds (employees at start of current quarter × productivity in the quarter),
>
> then overtime production = actual production less (employees at start of quarter × productivity)
>
> otherwise overtime production = zero.

Overtime pay (row 64): employees at the end of the previous quarter (row 61) × basic pay (row 51) × 0.5 × overtime production (row 63).

This is divided by: 0.25 × employees at the start of the quarter (row 61) × productivity (row 199), rounded to the nearest whole number.

Customer orders (row 65) are defined as row 54 if the appropriate cell in row 54 holds a number above zero, otherwise orders are as calculated in row 196. Note that row 66 shows 'A' if row 54 is zero (for actual orders), and 'E' otherwise (for estimated orders).

Sales (row 67) are given by the minimum of A and B where:

A = estimated orders (row 54) (if the contents of row 54 > 0, otherwise customer orders (row 65)

B = actual production (row 62) + finished goods stock at the end of the previous quarter (row 72)

Raw material stock (row 70) is given by:

raw material stock at the end of the previous quarter (row 70)
+ raw materials bought this quarter (row 43) (negative numbers ignored, and rounded to the nearest whole number)
− actual production this quarter (row 62)

Raw material cost (row 71) is copied from row 176.

Finished goods stock (row 72) is given by:

finished goods stock at the end of the previous quarter (row 72)
+ actual production (row 62)
− sales (row 67)

Finished goods cost (row 73) is copied from row 157.

Total stock value (row 74) is defined as:

raw material stock (row 70)
× raw material cost (row 71)
+ finished goods stock (row 72)
× finished goods cost (row 73)

Note that raw material stock is always valued at the current raw material unit cost. This ignores the possibility that some stock could have been purchased earlier at a lower cost and carried forward and avoids the need for more complex stock and inflation accounting methods.

Profit and loss (see Figure A1.6)

Please note that the cost of goods sold and the operating expenses are defined on the conventional business accounting basis. Costs which are directly associated with producing the finished product are included in the cost of goods sold. These include raw materials, labour, labour-related expenses and depreciation. Other costs, which are only indirectly associated with producing the finished product (i.e. 'overheads') are included in operating expenses. These include fixed overheads, advertising, recruitment and redundancy expenses and distribution costs.

This cost categorization is not synonymous with the distinction between fixed and variable costs. For example, cost of goods sold includes both raw materials (variable) and depreciation (fixed) costs. Participants may need to be encouraged to make their own analysis of the costs incurred by the business, for example estimating fixed and variable costs in order to aid discussion or to construct a 'break-even' chart.

Cumulative profit/ loss (row 201, not shown)

Row 201 accumulates losses or profits up to date. For example, in quarter two cell D201 shows a cumulative loss of £1996. This is composed of a loss of £3956 in quarter one and a profit of £1960 in quarter two.

Similarly, in quarter three E201 shows a cumulative profit of £313 and in quarter four cell F201 shows a cumulative loss of £4017. It is this cumulative profit or loss in quarter four which is taxable, so in this case no tax is due, as shown in cell F88. If a net profit had been earned over the first four quarters it would have been taxable at 30 per cent.

This loss is carried forward and offset against any future profit. Thus in the first quarter of year two, i.e. quarter five, cell G201 contains the following calculation:

> if the cumulative profit/loss in quarter four (cell F201) is positive (i.e. a profit was made over the first year as a whole), the cumulative profit in quarter five (cell G201) is equal to the net profit in quarter five (cell G86), and no reduction is made,

> if the cumulative profit/loss in quarter four is negative (i.e. a loss was made over the first year as a whole), then that loss is subtracted from any profit or loss made in quarter five, i.e. G201 is equal to G86 less the loss shown in F201.

A similar calculation occurs in cell K201 for quarter nine.

Suggested improvements

The following are a few suggestions for improving the simulation. The precise way in which these improvements could be carried out is left to the interested reader.

1 A loyalty bonus could be paid for employees who stay with the firm for more than a year. This would mean keeping two separate counts of employees, one with a length of service of up to four quarters, and one for employees with a length of service of five quarters or more. The usual wastage calculations could be made for both groups, and those employees 'surviving' to quarter five would receive the extra payment. An additional feature might be to assume that the longer service employees would leave at a slower rate than the new ones.

2 A second product group could be introduced, with a different demand level and cost. The same employees, materials and equipment could be used, but the product could perhaps suffer less seasonality than the first one. For simplicity the same productivity could apply to both products, and additional production and pricing decisions would be necessary.

3 A maximum overdraft limit could be introduced, beyond which the participant cannot go (the spreadsheet could easily show warning messages in this case!). The only complexity here is that if a macro is used to run the model, it would have to detect an excessive overdraft and offer the user an opportunity to change decisions, or the administrator would have to increase the loan (or decrease the loan or current account interest rate).

4. A quality element could be introduced into the production process (resulting in, say, a one-to-five 'star rating'). The quality could depend on pay relative to inflation (perhaps including overtime payments), and the previous quarter's service level. The result of improved quality would be an increase in market share for the same price, or the opportunity to charge a premium price.

Intervening in the simulation

Remind users that they should endeavour to keep their overdraft within £100 000 or any other level you consider reasonable, and that the loan is due for repayment in quarters five and nine. Also remind them of the various constraints on production and on sales.

You may introduce different economic conditions by changing data in row 187. Orders will respond in direct proportion to this row. You may also intervene by changing any data on the 'base data' screen, for example to change inflation rates or tax rates.

Note: before making any changes first make the data visible and unprotected as follows:

Use command /RFR to make the data visible and specify the range C167..N181 for the base data, or C187..N187 for the potential market size.

Use the command /RU to unprotect and refer to the same ranges.

After entering the required changes, reverse the process to hide and protect the data. Use the command /RFH to hide the data and /RP to protect it.

After making any changes to the spreadsheet, do not forget to resave the spreadsheet before returning it to participants.

Loans

The administrator may make changes to the loans granted or repaid by entering appropriate information in row 167. Note that loans need not be repaid in full by the end of the simulation.

Simulation suppliers and typical products

The information shown here was compiled from published literature and from discussions and correspondence with simulation designers and suppliers. The list is by no means comprehensive, but is believed to include many of the better-known UK suppliers together with examples of their products. Several major US suppliers and simulations are described and there is a less complete account of suppliers from selected European countries. The UK section includes suppliers specializing in computer-based or manual simulations and those offering simulations as part of wider consultancy or training services. Other sections only list suppliers of computer-based simulations.

The United Kingdom Alameda Software Ltd, Friern Lodge, The Avenue, Ampthill, Bedford, MK45 2NR.

Alameda supplies EXECUTIVE TEAM BUSINESS GAME, a well-established, computerized simulation providing participants with experience of various interactions within a company. It has been used by many organizations including polytechnics and business schools. The simulation encourages team development and objective setting. It helps to reinforce financial knowledge and can be run with between two and twenty teams, usually from five to twelve periods.

The simulation is also suitable for in-company use as it is sufficiently flexible to allow a degree of tailoring for a particular context and for various levels of ability and experience. It has a number of special features including strikes, increased material costs or wages, negotiation issues and changes in taxation.

April Computing Ltd, Chestnut Farm, Tarvin Rd, Frodsham, Cheshire, WA6 6XN.

April Computing was formed in 1985 and specializes in the design and production of a range of computerized business simulations. Up to

100 000 students and managers are trained each year and April also provide a tailor-made service. Several simulations have significant self-customization potential. April provide a telephone 'hotline' and a user group for discussion among simulation users. Simulations include the CAR 100 simulation, especially suitable for the motor industry, and other simulations developed from it.

EXECUTIVE is a simulation of the Western European or North American Motor Industry, which has recently been amended to take account of the recent downturn in world car sales. The simulation is available in three formats. In EXECUTIVE 100, teams enter decisions on a decision sheet and the administrator enters these into the computer. In EXECUTIVE 200 the administrator can modify the market data, and in EXECUTIVE 300 teams have the use of a what-if? model. EXECUTIVE can handle up to nine teams of four to ten people and the simulation can be expanded to provide additional modules, for example to represent the stock market, or to focus on quality issues. In addition to corporate users, a junior version of EXECUTIVE is also available for schools and colleges.

Daedal Training, 309 High St., Orpington, Kent, BR6 ONN.

Daedal has 20 years' experience of supplying a wide range of ready-to-use management training activities including in-tray exercises, mazes and business games. Uses include communications and people management skills, time management, telephone skills, health and safety, customer relations and disciplinary skills. They also provide a tailor-made service for a number of prominent companies. For business and management uses the company supplies a number of computer and manually-based simulations.

A.I.S. Debenham, 9 Roland Way, London, SW7 3RF.

A.I.S. Debenham designs simulations for team-building purposes and also numerically-oriented ones for learning about running a business. He also consults in training and management development and has run workshops in the UK and Hong Kong. Most simulations have been published in *Design Your Own Business Games* and *A Handbook of Management Training Exercises* by BACIE.

Peter Dye Associates, The Old Vicarage, Chiddingly, East Sussex, BN8 6HE.

Peter Dye Associates design computer-based simulations for their own use and for clients. IMPPACT! was originally developed in association with the Institute of Personnel Managers, and is a computer-based simulation in which up to six teams can take part, making a range of decisions over six or twelve months. Each month teams have to make five to ten decisions about a series of incidents. The unusual feature of IMPPACT! is the 60 case studies designed to illustrate the link between personnel decisions and business performance. These relate to recruitment, training, disciplinary and industrial relations problems. Most of these could be used independently of the simulation.

REPUTABLE MERCHANTS LTD is an interactive trading simulation focusing on such areas as business analysis and objective setting, pricing and product mix, stock, cost and cash control and the use of market information.

WINWIN is a very realistic commercial negotiation simulation reflecting the differing levels of trading performance that result from varying approaches to the preparation and implementation phases of negotiation.

THE SUPER STOCKING COMPANY is a simulation illustrating how the materials management function can contribute to company performance. It provides a practical framework for forecasting, stock scheduling, and purchasing decision making. Re-order quantities and levels, discount breaks, emergency purchasing and stockholding costs all play their part.

Edit 515 Ltd, 24 Buckstone Grove, Edinburgh, EH10 6PF.

Edit 515 has 21 years' experience in computer-based business simulations. The company developed the Scotsman Management Game and has run it for the last 20 years. The emphasis is on customer service rather than selling standard products. Exports are now 30–35 per cent of income, and originate from many countries including Australia, Brazil, the CIS and Zimbabwe.

Activities include the design of tailor-made simulations for such companies as Ford Europe. This is a detailed simulation of a Ford dealership used as the basis of training courses over the last eight years. Another example is the simulation of a Cooperative Society now under development for the Cooperative movement, and tailored versions of standard products for Kodak, Bowater and Texaco.

Standard products have been sold to companies such as Bowater, Texaco, British Gas and Natwest. The company also runs courses in which software is a key element, and is involved in competitions with the Welsh Management Game, and a game for the Institute of Management Services. They license software for competitions abroad and other activities include running statistics courses.

Chris Elgood Associates, Abacus House, Cranbrook Rd, Hawkhurst, Kent, TN18 4AR.

Chris Elgood produces and distributes a wide range of management games and simulations, including computer-based ones available for IBM and BBC computers. Computer-based simulations are provided in many different subject areas and for all types of participants, from undergraduates to senior managers, working either individually or in teams. The games are divided into three categories, people-skill games, management games and business games.

THE VALUE OF T is a people-skill game involving leadership, problem solving and cooperation for six to twelve people. The equipment for the game consists of a pack of cards which are distributed among the group. Each card either contains a simple sum or an instruction to combine in some way the values on other cards. Collectively the cards contain the information needed to find the value of 'T', but only if players have a common understanding of the task, agree on how it should be tackled, and play their own part carefully. The game is relevant for all those in supervisory and management positions.

THE ORGANISATION GAME is a management game in which a number of tasks have to be performed by individuals. Players are divided into groups. Each task is awarded points and the winning group is the one with the highest score at the end. The tasks include creative, numerical, physical and judgemental activities. Some are 'succeed or fail', and others allow various levels of success. Groups first discuss their skills and interests, and plan who does what. Scoring is rapid and the game is suitable for any level of group.

FINANCIT is a simple computer-based business game for up to six teams of three to four members. Teams make and sell up to three products each having its own production line. Decisions include the quantity of each product to be manufactured each quarter, and the price. After each quarter, information on the price charged, units sold and the stock position is made known to all teams. The aim is to make enough profit to convince investors that the firm deserves re-financing over a five-year timescale. The game encourages the careful analysis of information, forecasting and financial planning. It is appropriate for supervisors and junior or middle managers and needs about three hours.

John Fripp Associates, 3 Milebush, Leighton Buzzard, Beds, LU7 7UB.

John Fripp became active in business simulations in 1974 and has designed and run many simulations for Ashridge Management College and for private clients. In addition to general simulations, he provides a specialist service designing and producing tailor-made business simulations for client companies. Recent clients and sponsors include ICI, Fairey, Workhouse Ltd, British Aerospace, Price Waterhouse, IBM and Bowring Marsh & Mclennan Ltd. Each simulation is produced specifically for the client organization and addresses their own key issues using appropriate language and style of management reporting. All simulations are designed for IBM compatible computers.

BROKER was developed for Bowring Marsh & Mclennan Ltd as a training simulation for senior managers. It represents the activities of several competing broking firms in a competitive market under changing economic conditions. The decisions are those which such a company would make in reality, and allow participants to attempt to develop their business in a number of ways. One is to develop a branch network, staffed by competent and trained personnel, offering a high standard of service to clients. The other is to look for suitable acquisition opportunities which are available from time to time. Participants have to decide whether acquisitions are right for them and how much they are worth.

NOTHING VENTURE NOTHING GAIN is a simulation under development in conjunction with Workhouse Productions, and is designed to show the problems faced by a small company. The simulation is based upon a real company and is designed for the higher education or small business market. The simulation covers around twelve years of operation, and apart from a core of routine decisions which are repeated each year, it is unusual in that the issues faced and the major decisions made by participants differ from year to year. These special issues include diversification into a new product line, the opportunity to acquire another company, the need to buy new and larger premises as the company grows, the need to satisfy bankers in order to secure any necessary loan, dealing with a recession, and how to reward long-serving and loyal employees.

STRATGAME was developed for a large international manufacturing company as a means of raising the awareness of its executives to a range of strategic issues. The simulation is unusual in that it represents four different companies, each one based upon a real company in the industry. Each company starts the exercise with a different size, product portfolio, geographical spread and profitability. Several countries and market sectors are represented. Additional features include a realistic product development cycle, distribution agreements between 'competitors', and several different currencies, exchange and inflation rates.

BGAME is a simulation focusing on purchasing and inventory control activities. It also includes the full range of business functions associated with a manufacturing company, but is unusual in allowing face-to-face negotiations between supplier and purchaser. On the basis of their preparation for and conduct of the negotiation, teams can be awarded supplies at a specified cost, for several periods of the simulation, with or without guaranteed delivery, and with specified quality. The simulation produces a full set of results and accounts which highlight the bottom-line effect of the negotiations. Inflation and economic cycles also have to be dealt with.

INTERSIM is a simple simulation of a manufacturing company developed for junior management or higher education. The simulation contains many of the issues faced by a real business, including the need to operate a company within limited resources (financial, human and time), in the face of competition and a changing and uncertain business environment. The simulation is quick to run and produces simple accounts.

Hendry Training & Consultancy, Gobles Court, 7 Market Square, Bicester, Oxon, OX6 7AA.

Hendry Training designs training and consultancy activities to help clients address a range of critical issues essential to their future. These often involve the enhancement of both individual and organizational performance management, and are achieved through leading edge developments in thinking combined with enjoyable learning methods. Hendry helps people to learn using a variety of methods, including non-computer-based games and exercises using both indoor and outdoor activities.

The PADZ business game involves three separate parts of a company making pads to a given specification. The three parts are the Board, Factory Control and Factory Operations. The finished products are ordered by game control, and must be delivered to game control by an agreed time. They are made by Factory Operations using simple materials. The three parts of the company are situated in separate locations and the participants must organize themselves as they wish, developing roles and responsibilities in order to manufacture pads profitably. The exercise allows up to eighteen participants and is easy to administer and brief. It generates a wide range of behaviours which either consolidate learning at the end of a course, or provide reference points at the start of a course.

Human Synergistics-Verax, 60 High St, Odiham, Hampshire, RG25 1LN.

Human Synergistics is a company of management consultants that gives a full consultancy and training service and provides materials for organizations to use themselves, including both tailor-made and off-the-shelf games and simulations. A number of 'survival' exercises are available, including CASCADES, a mountain survival problem designed to help groups learn problem solving, team effectiveness and interpersonal skills. Materials include a booklet for each individual, a leader's manual and observers' guides.

Other exercises include DESERT SURVIVAL, SUB-ARCTIC SURVIVAL and JUNGLE SURVIVAL. A number of others are available focusing on problem solving, negotiation skills and influencing strategies.

Management Games Ltd, Methwold House, Northwold Rd, Methwold, Thetford, Norfolk IP26 4PF.

Founded in 1963, MGL provides some 500 management training resources, including packages used for leadership, communication skills, sales and marketing, grievance handling, teamworking and many other topics. Business simulations include both manual and computer-based types.

Their best selling business simulation is TYCOON, available in both manual and computer-based versions. This represents a company manufacturing a hypothetical consumer durable product in the year 2021. The simulation lasts from four to ten rounds, and in each round participants have to make a range of decisions on pricing, promotion, wage levels, etc. One interesting feature of the simulation is that participants do not need to make the full set of decisions each round. If decisions are not made, 'standard' decisions are applied, which are stored in the computer. MGL provides other computer-based simulations and a tailor-made service to clients.

Management Learning Resources Ltd, PO Box 28, Carmarthen, Dyfed, SA31 1DT.

MLR was incorporated in 1986 and produces and distributes management training and development materials and provides a consultancy service. Products include training guides and materials in a range of subjects including sales management, leadership, stress management and teambuilding, as well as management books and games. MLR is the exclusive European distributor for a wide range of simulation providers from the UK, Europe and the USA. It provides a wide range of manual games and simulations mostly in leadership and teambuilding areas.

ALASKAN ADVENTURE is a teamworking exercise in which teams are asked to imagine that a weekend fishing trip in Alaska has gone badly wrong when their boat sinks, leaving them in fear of their lives. Participants have to rank order, individually and then in teams, ten items salvaged from the boat. The expert ranking is provided by Alaskan bush pilots with many years of experience flying in Alaskan conditions. The exercise is very useful as a teambuilding device for new groups, or as a refresher or icebreaker.

THE HAT FACTORY is a game in which players work in teams to set up and operate a hat factory. Orders are received for three different styles in four colours and teams must decide which orders to fulfil and how to do so. The game is played over six simulated days and teams have to decide how to sequence orders, assign responsibilities, order supplies and prepare production schedules. The game is provided with full equipment and documentation.

Management Training Services Ltd, 14 Clayton Meadows, Bourne End, Bucks, SL8 5DQ.

Management Training Services is a small consultancy specializing in finance for non-financial managers and business simulation exercises. The two partners began their association while responsible for the diploma in Management Studies at Slough College of Higher Education. They have developed over 50 simulations and rather than sell the simulations, prefer to sell a package with themselves as trainers. These cover a wide range of industries, including consumer durables, small manufacturing, retailing, transport, car rental, television rental, the motor trade, printing, construction and many others. A number of tailor-made simulations have been produced, and simulations are now computer-based using a spreadsheet.

Northgate Training, 29 James St West, Bath, BA1 2BT.

Northgate Training designs and markets its own computer-based simulations. One of these, PIZZA PANIC is a group exercise which can be played by up to four teams. It is targeted at junior to senior management and lasts around three hours or can be run periodically over a longer period. The simulation is concerned with bidding for a site for a potential pizza take-away. Teams receive market research information, and the cost of advertising and running each site. They then have to make a number of decisions including what quality of pizza to produce and what price to charge. Additional team tasks include the production of a sample advertisement, the quality of which is judged by the trainer.

Pavic Publications, Department of Educational Services, Sheffield City Polytechnic, 36 Collegiate Crescent, Sheffield, S10 2BP.

Pavic has been publishing tape/slides, games, books, videos and computer software for many years. Most are designed by lecturers at the Polytechnic and are tailor-made for their courses. Pavic then makes the exercises available for sale to individuals and institutions. They are designed by teachers for teachers. Their most successful products are teaching packages, computer software, games for schools and children with learning difficulties, and workbooks for small firms.

SMG (Strategic Management Group Inc), 6 Heddon Street, London, W1R 7HL.

SMG was founded in 1981 at the Wharton School in the USA and has developed an internationally-recognized management consulting, development and training organization. They now have several offices in the USA and also in seven other countries. SMG is organized into several industry-specific areas and offers specialist consulting, seminars, simulations and computer-based training. SMG also has a research and development team in the USA, numbering around 25 people, working on simulations. They have developed tailor-made simulations for companies such as Sears Roebuck, Hewlett Packard, Motorola and Ford. They also customize simulations for particular clients and 'localize' simulations for different markets in Europe.

The company offers two types of simulations, the normal type involving quantitative decisions, and scenario-based simulations dealing with the behavioural aspects of management. One of the best known of the scenario-based simulations is THE COMPLETE PROJECT MANAGER. This is based on research into the major factors that contribute to project success or failure. It represents a computer software company that is developing a new product. In the simulation a project team has been set up and participants have to manage the team and its relationships with key stakeholders in order to develop the software to a high quality, on time and budget, and maintain the confidence of its management. Each quarter teams have to face a number of key scenarios. Each gives a choice of three or four options. In order to gather information and impressions, participants have the opportunity to listen to the 'grapevine' in various parts of the organization, and to hold 'meetings' with key people. A key issue is how to satisfy the needs of the client, boss and other team members and stakeholders who all play a vital role in the project. At the end of each round of three months, participants receive extensive feedback, summarizing the issues under debate during the quarter, the decisions that were taken and the effects of those decisions. They also receive a stakeholder report, showing the team score and management satisfaction, and a project report indicating the quality of the product under development, the financial status and Gannt chart. The simulation can be run as part of a three-day or longer course.

Solent Simulations Ltd, 22 Hamilton Close, Southbrook Rd, Havant, Hants, PO9 1RP.

Solent is a firm of consultants which designs and supplies its own manual games and simulations. These include a range of board and card games and simulations for use in education and training. Also included are a number of role-playing exercises, an example of which is 'Me—The Slow Learner', designed to give people the experience of having difficulties in learning. This is used mainly in the teaching, nursing and caring professions but is also relevant to personnel management.

Stainton Associates, Mariners House, High St, Hamble, Hampshire, SO3 5JF.

Established in 1983 by Professor Roy Stainton, Stainton Associates has become a leading firm of consultants in marketing, strategic management and business systems. Successful associations with management centres and 'blue chip' companies have encouraged the recent acquisition of the Swiss Management Consultancy Association Abegglen UK Limited. The new company, Stainton Abbeglen, concentrates on management consultancy, while Stainton Associates continues to expand in business systems and management training. The obvious synergy that now exists throughout the company is an excellent foundation for activities throughout Europe.

Stainton Abegglen is involved in a number of related activities, including the development of information technology for sales and marketing planning, computer-aided decision making, the design of bespoke business simulations, assessment centres and training in marketing, sales and business awareness. Stainton Abegglen will develop tailor-made versions of any simulation for other companies. The following are a selection of recent business simulations.

HUBS was developed for IBM and can be run over three days. It is directed at training managers in the electrical, computer and instrument engineering industries.

AMSAT was developed for ICI Agrochemicals and reflects the issues facing marketing managers in the pesticides business.

ESTEEM was developed with Eagle Star Insurance Company and allows local and national marketing, including many features of the insurance industry.

MARSIM is centred on the confectionary manufacturing and retailing business. It has been run successfully with a number of companies.

Strategic People, Pepys House, 48 Station Rd, Chertsey, Surrey, KT16 8BE.

Strategic People focuses on the delivery of strategic and business plans through the people employed in an organization. They do this by dealing with the mechanistic aspect of planning, manpower, management succession and skills deployment, and also with the culture of the organization, or 'how we do things around here'. They have a number of tried and tested tools to aid the planning process, and are the originators of DILEMMA!, a board game which encourages participants to explore issues of culture, values and business ethics. The game involves a journey around a board during which participants come up against a number of dilemmas. This can be used in a variety of ways—for strategy seminars for senior managers or to reinforce or explore corporate culture.

The company also runs a number of tailor-made courses and offers consultancy focusing on a range of human resource issues, including teamworking, managing change, recruitment and selection and performance management.

Strat*X, Vicarage House, 58–60 Kensington High St, London, W8 4DB. See USA entry for details.

Total Business Services, 29 Hollow Way Lane, Amersham, Bucks, HP6 6DJ.

Total Business Services provides a range of accounting, financial, legal and secretarial services, and the management game SEMINAR which has been used by a variety of prominent companies.

SEMINAR is a computerized production management exercise involving the deployment of money and physical resources in order to maximize profits. There are a number of decisions to be made each month, including manufacturing, personnel and marketing ones. When results are returned they contain full accounts for the team concerned and information on other companies. The package is IBM compatible and contains 10 participant's manuals, an instructor's manual and other information. The company also tailors products to users' specific requirements.

Understanding (Systems) Ltd, 28 Orchard Avenue, Finchley, London, N3 3NL.

Understanding (Systems) has specialized for a number of years in the development of management training simulations. One of its main products is PLAN IT, a product that has gone through several stages of development and the current pc version is PLAN IT EXECUTIVE.

PLAN IT requires up to 12 decisions covering finance, sales and production. Extensive management reports and graphs are produced, and around 400 help screens are available to explain how the simulation works as well as basic business concepts. The simulation is very flexible and the trainer can change the simulation parameters to suit any particular purpose. It can be used for financial skills training, for general management purposes to integrate a range of topics and for teambuilding purposes. Understanding (Systems) Ltd also acts as distributor for an American software house specializing in banking simulations, varying in sophistication and suitable for a range of banking employees from entry level to senior banking executives.

Wessex Training Services, 5 Acorn Business Centre, Tower Park, Poole, BH12 4NZ.

Wessex Training Services is both a resource centre and a training consultancy. As a resource centre it has an extensive range of training materials including videos, flexible learning materials, computer-based training and interactive videos, games and simulations. The simulations are produced by a number of other well-known suppliers. As training consultants Wessex design creative training activities which fit into the context of the organization and individuals concerned. An example is the TOWER OF BABEL, an exercise focusing on problem-solving skills, planning, communication and teamwork. The task is to relocate the Tower of Babel, an ancient tower built from six huge blocks. A model is available for each team to work out how to move the tower, one piece at a time, obeying certain simple rules, and paying penalties if the rules are broken (for example, if a move takes more than a certain length of time, or if more than one person touches the same block). Each team acts as a group of civil engineers asked to quote for the removal of the tower. They all have to try and win the contract and make a profit in so doing.

Austria   Peter M. Hartel, Steirische Volkswirtschaftliche, Freiheitplatz, 2/III, A 8010 Graz, Austria.

OKOTOPIA represents the complex interactions between different sections of society in Austria, and includes economic and ecological issues. Various groups are involved including industry (production, employees, environmental facilities), agriculture and forestry (fertilization and deforestation issues), trade, crafts and tourism (output, employment, prices, environmental issues) and households (private consumption, housing space, citizens' actions, wage negotiations, traffic, energy use, waste production).

Posters are used to announce news, conferences are held, negotiations take place, then decisions are entered into the computer. The game runs for two or three days and results include national economic data, measures of quality of life, and conditions in the region.

France   J-C Larreche, Insead, Fontainbleau, France.

Larreche and others have developed a number of sophisticated marketing simulations including MARKSTRAT, MARKOPS and INDUSTRAT, which is the industrial marketing version of Markstrat. Many of these are distributed through Strat*X (see below).

Strat*X sa, European Head Office, 73 rue Victor Hugo, 77250 Veneux les Sablons, France. See USA entries for details.

Germany   A survey carried out in Germany in 1985 on management games recorded 250 management games in use in German-speaking countries. About 200 dealt with the enterprise or part of it, the others focusing on social, political or ecological problems. The majority of games were computer based and were used both in universities and for management training. Simulation is an accepted management training tool in Germany, and many prominent companies take part in business simulations. For example, Bayer has trained over 5000 managers using games. In 1986 Rohn reported a growing demand for more clearly differentiated games, particularly those which deal with the problems of smaller companies or specific industries. The following is a sample of some of the better known games.

Bundeszentrale für politische Bildung, Referat 'Neue Median', Berliner Freiheit 7, D 5300 Bonn 1, Germany.

KOMMSTED is a decision-making game in parliamentary democracy. It was jointly developed by the Bundeszentrale für politische Bildung (Federal Centre for Political Education) and the German National Research Centre for Computer Science. Participants take the roles of government and opposition party members, an employers' association, entrepreneurs, trade unionists and private citizens. Software tools include a database allowing access to relevant information, a word processor, computerized production of results, graphics and comprehensive written materials. The game needs an IBM 386 and 10Mb hard disc. Two to five networked terminals are recommended for multi-use of software.

M. Grutz, Fachhochschule Konstanz, Department of Computer Science, Brauneggerstrasse 55, 7750 Konstanz, Germany.

KLIMA-NET (Klinik Management) was developed for training decision making in hospitals. Originally developed in 1975, it has had many additions and improvements since. Patient input and length of stay are probabilistic. Over 12 periods players have to make decisions in capacity use, manpower planning, investment and operating expenses. Results include cost per case, profit/loss and quality of care.

Munich Centre for Advanced Training in Applied Statistics for Developing Countries, Carl Duisberg Gesellschaft e. V., Pfalzer-Wald Str.2, D-800, Munchen 90, Germany.

HARAMBEE, the simulation described in Chapter 8, was developed by the Munich Centre and the Food Studies Group at Queen Elizabeth House, University of Oxford. It was created for training key decision makers in developing countries and to facilitate mutual understanding between providers and users of information.

H. Weber, USW, Schloss Gracht, 5042 Erftstraft 1 (Liblar), Germany.

MARGA simulates a manufacturing company with three products in four markets, in Germany, the EC, the USA and the Far East. USW (Universitätsseminar der Wirtschaft) in Cologne has run a national simulation competition for some years, attracting around 300 teams from German business. In 1991 and 1992 an international competition took place using MARGA, the first of its kind, with teams from top international companies from the UK, Germany, France and Spain. The contest was run in collaboration with major business periodicals and national daily newspapers in England, France and Germany.

MARGA is claimed to be among the hardest and most complex management training exercises in Germany. It was developed over 20 years ago and over 45 000 managers from 2000 companies have participated in the simulation from Germany as a whole. Decision areas include marketing, finance, human resources, research, production and distribution. Optional computer modelling facilities are available. An English version also exists. The training objective is to 'exercise interactive thought processes and promote the capability to coordinate and harmonise the divergent interests in a corporation, towards a common long term, strategic goal'.

W. Schuit, Lernsysteme, Postfach 1805, D4432, Gronau, Germany.

KOSTKAL is a good example of a simple game with very few decisions, comprising the selling prices for one or two products. The main learning goals are to do with costing, inflation and business cycles. Stock fluctuations and the purchase and depreciation of machinery can also be included.

Siemens Nixdorf Computer AG, Anna Birle-Str. 9, D 6503, Mainz-Kastel, Germany.

TOPSIM is a general management game whose training aims include the formulation of goals and strategies, the transformation of these into operations, diagnosis and action on critical situations, a better understanding of business economics and the use of microcomputers in business.

The Netherlands The Institute For Training in Intercultural Management B.V., Celebesstraat 96, 2585 TP Den Haag, The Netherlands.

The Institute for Training in Intercultural Management (ITIM) was founded in 1985 as an offshoot of the Institute for Research on Intercultural Cooperation (IRIC), whose director is Geert Hofstede. The two institutes cooperate closely. ITIM provides simulations, but these are embedded in training courses and cannot be used separately. Some are off-the-shelf and others have been developed specially for clients.

USA In 1961 there were estimated to be about 100 business games in existence in the USA, and by that time over 30 000 business executives had used them (Kibbee *et al*, 1961). By 1980 there were over 200 simulations (Horn and Cleaves, 1980). There are probably now more business simulations and games in use in the USA than in any other country in the world. Many designers produce excellent simulations and user guides, often charging little or nothing for the software.

J. R. Barker, C. S. Temple and H. M. Cloan, 33 Hayden St., Lexington, MA, USA.

The WORLDWIDE SIMULATION EXERCISE has recently been revised and is one of the most popular simulations dealing with international business. Two products are produced from a head office in the USA, and there are between 30 and 40 decisions per period. Up to seven teams can take part.

W. R. Hoskins, Phoenix, Arizona, USA, American Graduate School of Business.

The MULTINATIONAL BUSINESS GAME is one of the strongest international business simulations, focusing on a wide range of international issues including hedging, foreign currency speculation, foreign exchange and trade barriers. There are 15 options for expansion into different countries, including options to produce close to their markets, in low cost countries, or make use of tariff barriers. Teams also have to cope with problems arising from political unrest, multiple currencies and inflation. There are usually eight to twelve quarters of operation and up to nine teams are allowed.

B. Keys, A. Edge, A. and W. Remus have THE MULTINATIONAL MANAGEMENT GAME, published by Richard D. Irwin, Homewood, IL, USA.

The latest version of this simulation was produced in 1992. There can be three to seven participants per team and between two and eight teams competing in producing microcomputers and related equipment. Three geographical areas are covered; North America, Asia and Europe, although the simulation can be played purely domestically within the USA. Teams may export from the USA or set up production facilities in other countries. It provides equal focus on marketing, manufacturing and finance and there are also human resource decisions. It may be played for between five and fifteen yearly periods. Sixteen decisions are required for the North American market and twelve or fourteen for other markets. Players may input their decisions on a paper form or via discs. A series of planning sheets is available to encourage a rational decision process. Data are provided on each of the national markets and the game is suitable for strategic management and international management courses. There is a participant's and administrator's manual.

H. R. Preismeyer, South Western Publishing Co.,Cincinatti, USA.

STRATEGY! aims to cover both strategic and tactical aspects of managing a business. Up to 20 teams can own several companies in any of 10 different industries and each team member can manage one or more of the companies. Companies can be bought or sold, and created or liquidated. Each quarter an 'environmental report' is available covering technological and demographic changes, weather conditions and foreign competition. New reports can be created by the administrator.

The 10 industries are quite different, and include a lawnmower manufacturer, a diaper service, toy retailing, cellular telephones, mineral exploration and videotape rental. The simulation manual includes one-page descriptions of each industry. Quarterly decisions are made and decisions for each strategic business unit include sales, cost of goods sold, overheads, advertising and R&D budgets, buying or selling plant and equipment, and depreciation, all in $s. Overdrafts are also available. The software includes a disc for the administrator and a decision disc, which is a spreadsheet for forecasting and budgeting and for transferring decisions to the administrator and giving reports to participating teams.

J. R. Smith and P. A. Golden, University of Louisville, USA.

CORPORATION is a business strategy simulation published in 1989 by Prentice Hall, Englewood Cliffs, New Jersey. It is based on a multi-divisional, multinational company in the electronic information systems industry. There are 13 corporate decisions and eight decisions for each strategic business unit. Business unit decisions include prices, salesforce size, production and R&D budget. Corporate decisions include the type and size of a strategic business unit, bank loan, buying or selling a business unit, and entering into a number of new ventures.

After each period of six months a written 'incident' is presented and teams have to make a choice from several options. Choices are entered into the simulation. Up to 12 teams may participate. There is a participant's and administrator's manual.

Strat*X International, 222 Third Street, Cambridge, MA 02142, USA.

For some years Strat*X has distributed MARKSTRAT, one of the best known simulations. The simulation focuses on product portfolio, market segmentation and product positioning. It provides graphical representation of customers' needs and perceptions and a decision support system. Developed by Jean-Claude Larreche, Professor of Marketing at Insead, the rights have now been transferred to Strat*X. Up to five competing teams manufacture and market initially two brands of a consumer durable. Decisions are entered either on decision forms or via a disc. Decisions relate to production, advertising, market research, price, and numbers of salesmen. The market is divided into five segments and a set of up to 15 market research studies are available. Additional decisions allow other brands to be launched, or existing ones to be withdrawn. Brands can be positioned and repositioned with respect to the needs of various consumer segments. Markstrat also has two other variations, MARKSTRAT-INDUSTRIAL, for companies marketing goods to other firms, and MARKSTRAT PHARMACEUTICAL, which is currently under development. This will focus on strategic allocation of resources, market segmentation, product positioning and competitive analysis. It includes typical pharmaceutical marketing issues in an international environment.

A later simulation is MARKOPS, designed to allow non-marketing specialists to appreciate more fully that other functions have responsibilities for satisfying customer needs. There are parts to play for product development, manufacturing, sales and finance functions. The simulation is available for IBM computers, complete with a 200 page manual and 600 graphs which are available at the touch of a key. The main marketing concepts include marketing operations (pricing, sales force, technical and sales support, credit terms, etc.), market segmentation strategy, allowing allocation of resources across several segments, product positioning strategy, and product portfolio strategy.

Strat*X is willing to adapt simulations to customers' needs or develop new ones.

H. Thorelli, School of Business, Indiana University, Bloomington, IN 47405, USA.

INTOP simulates international business operations and the previous version had 100 users around the world. Special features include high technology products, foreign currency, strategic alliances, joint ventures, and special 'host country' relationships. A new version is being planned for publication in 1992. The simulation also involves either division into manufacturing and wholesaling or a fully integrated company. There are industrial and consumer products and negotiation takes place between parties. Unlimited numbers of decisions and environmental events are allowed, including inflation, devaluation and different trade policies. Any one of 800 parameters can be set by a few keystrokes.

Computing requirements are stringent, including the need for an IBM AT or compatible, 640k RAM and 20Mb hard disc. A Hewlett Packard Laserjet printer or equivalent is desirable for speed of printout.

Yugoslavia   Little use has been made of business simulations or, until recently, any form of training based upon Western concepts of demand-supply management. One of the few management educators to make use of simulations is Professor Janko Kralj, Univerza V Mariboru, Ekonomsko-Poslovna Fakulteta, Maribor, Slovenia (Yugoslavia), who has used simulations and has written extensively about the merits of case studies and business simulations and the problems faced by companies making the transition to a genuine market economy. He sees an important place for both case studies and business games in this process.

Index

Containing subjects, references, and names of games and simulations. (Names of games and simulations are shown thus: *ITALICS*.)

ABSEL, 123
Acquisitions, 5–6
Action learning, 45
Action mazes, 20
Administrator's guide to a Simulation, example of, 147–161
Alameda Software, 162
ALASKAN ADVENTURE, 168
AMSAT, 170
Anderson, R. A., 20
April Computing, 162–163
Argyris, C., 52
Ashridge, 1, 115

Barker, J. R., 174
Bateson, G., 38
Belbin, R. M., 111, 118
BGAME, 166
British Aerospace, 110–111
BROKER, 165
Bowen, K. C., 117
Bundeszentrale fur politische Bildung, 173
Burgess, T. F., 32
Business simulations:
  benefits of, 34–35
  characteristics of, 20–22
  complexity and realism of, 31
  computer-based, 24, 26–32
  constraints in, 21
  decision aids used in, 31
  differences among, 23–32
  disadvantages of, 35–36, 49–50
  environment of, 21
  focus of, 30
  goals in, 20
  interactions in, 30
  model-based, 26–32
  off-the-shelf, 56–58
  participants in, 30
  price, representation of, 26–27
  results achieved in, 21
  scenario-based, 29
  scope of, 31
  tailor-made, 56–58
  timescale of, 30
  type of results of, 31
  use of nomogram in, 26–27

CAR 100, 163
CASCADES, 167
Case studies:
  as methods of learning, 51–54
  describing the use of simulations, 110–124
Choosing a simulation, 56–58
CLUG, 20
Coaching and counselling, 47
Competences, 42–44
THE COMPLETE PROJECT MANAGER, 169
Constructs, 39
COPE, 78
CORPORATION, 176
Coyle, R. G., 74

Daedal Training, 163
Debenham, A. I. S., 163
Decisions in simulations, 3, 6, 59, 65, 126
DESERT SURVIVAL, 167
Designing a simulation:
  cause-effect tables in, 74
  concept of, 65–67
  constraints in, 3
  economic conditions represented in, 2, 4, 65

example in the furniture manufacturing industry, 84–96
financial aspects of, 77
ideal process, 59–60
influence diagrams in, 71–73, 75
managing the project, 62–63
operational aspects of, 77
personnel issues in, 4
process, 55–83
programming, 77–79
prototyping in, 61, 75, 78–79
qualitative model underlying, 67–73
quantitative model underlying, 73–77
roles in, 62
tailor-made, 58–83
by a team, 2–3, 55
testing and validation, 79–82
working methods, 62–63
DILEMMA!, 171
Dye, P., Associates, 163

Eden, C., Jones, S. and Sims, D., 69
Edit 515, 164
Elgood, Chris, Associates, 123, 164
ESTEEM, 170
EXECUTIVE, 163
EXECUTIVE TEAM BUSINESS GAME, 162
Experiential learning, 39–42

Faria, A. J., 32
Financial simulations, 17–18
FINANCIT, 165
Flight simulator, 8–10
Freeman, J., 99
Fripp, John, and Associates, 33, 165–166

Games, *see* Simulations
GAMMA, 78
Garratt, R., 38
Gentry, J. W., 123
Gladstein, D. L., and Reilly, N. P., 120
Gooding, C., 100
Greenblat, C. S., 123
Grutz, M., 173

Hammond, J. S., 59
HARAMBEE, 173
Hartel, P. M., 172
THE HAT FACTORY, 168
Hendry Training and Consultancy, 166

Honey, R., and Mumford, A., 41
Horn, R. E., and Cleaves, A., 32, 123
Hoskins, W. R., 175
HUBS, 170
Human Synegistics–Verax, 167

IBM, 38
IMPPACT!, 163
Influence diagrams, 71–73, 75
INTERSIM, 166
IThink, 78
INTOP, 177
The Institute for Training in Intercultural Management, 174
In-tray exercises, 20
ISAGA, 124

Jacobs, R. L., and Baum, M., 32
Jones, K., 123
JUNGLE SURVIVAL, 167

Kaplan, R. E., 117
Kelly, G. A., 39
Keys, J. B., 124
    and Edge, A., and Remus, W., 175
    and Wolfe, J., 117
Kibbee, J. M., Craft, C. J., and Nanus, B., 124
Klein, R. D., and Fleck, R. A., 124
KLIMA–NET, 173
Kolb, D. A., 39
KOMMSTED, 173
KOSTKAL, 174
Kralj, J., 177

Larreche, J–C., 172
Larreche, J–C., and Gatignon, H., 124
Larreche, J–C., and Weinstein, D., 124
Learning:
    event, design of, 40
    cerebral, 38
    methods, 1, 44–54
        action learning, 45–47
        action mazes, 20
        case studies, 51–54
        coaching and counselling, 47
        comparisons between, 53–54
        lectures, 52–54
        on-the-job, 45
        outdoor management development, 50–51
        resource centre, 47

simulations, 48–50, 53–54
Organization, the, 38
skills, 39
theory, 39–42
transformational, 39
Learning organizations, 38
Lectures, 52–54
Lombardo, M., McCall, M., and de
Vries, D., 116

Magistrates clerks, management training
of, 115–116
Management Games Ltd., 167
Management learning resources, 167
Management training services, 168
Manually operated simulations, 18–20
MARGA, 173
MARKOPS, 176–177
MARKSTRAT, 176
MARSIM, 170
McKenna, R. J., 32
McKenney, J. L., 53
Me—the Slow Learner, 19, 170
Models, 8
Model-based simulations, 26–29
Moore, C. M., 69
Moutinho, L., 53
*THE MULTINATIONAL BUSINESS
GAME*, 175
*THE MULTINATIONAL MANAGEMENT
GAME*, 175
The Munich Centre for Advanced
Training in Applied Statistics
for Developing Countries, 173

NASAGA, 123
Negotiations during a simulation, 110–
111
Nomograms, 19, 26–27
Northgate Training, 168
NOTHING VENTURE, NOTHING GAIN,
165–166

OKOTOPIA, 172
On-the-job learning, 45
THE ORGANIZATION GAME, 165
Osigweh, C. A. B., 52
Outdoor management development,
50–51

PADZ, 167
Participant's guide to a simulation,

example of, 125–147
Pavic Publications, 169
Pedler, M., Burgoyne, J., and Boydell, T.,
44
PIZZA PANIC, 168
PLAN IT, 171
Preismeyer, H. R., 175
Progressive games and simulations, 29

Raia, P. A. A., 53
REPUTABLE MERCHANTS LTD, 164
Resource centre learning, 47
Risk analysis, 17–18
Research uses of simulations, 117–121
Rohn, W. E., 124
Running a simulation:
administrator's roles in, 23, 41, 97–99
administrator's guide, example of,
147–161
analysis and planning during, 102–
103
as part of a course, 1
briefing for, 102
choosing winners after, 107
debriefing after, 106–107
decision aids in, 108
decision submission during, 103
feedback during, 104–105
nomograms used for, 19, 26–27
objective setting within, 104
practical arrangements for, 108
preparation for, 98–99
presentation of results of, 103–104
reflection during, 104
trial run of, 5
sustaining interest within, 105–106
team selection for, 99
teamwork in, 103
types of use, 99–100
what can go wrong during, 109

SAGSET, 124
Schuit, W., 174
SEMINAR, 171
Sharda, R. M., Barr, S. H., and
McDonnell, J. C., 120
Siemens Nixdorf Computer, 174
SIMULA, 77
Simulation and gaming, 123
Simulations/games for learning, 124
Simulations:
behavioural, 16–17, 22, 116

benefits of, 6–7, 48–50
business, 23–37
case studies describing the use of, 110–124
deterministic, 22
documentation for, 6, 82–83, 125–161
examples of:
  for dock design, 10
  in the furniture manufacturing industry, 84–96
  in the insurance industry, 1–7, 15
  for manpower planning, 15–16, 22
  for production plant design, 8
  for the assessment of project profitability, 8
  for research purposes, 117–121
  for the development and testing of business policy, 2, 111–113
  for the design of a telephone exchange, 11–15
financial, 17–18
operational, 10–16, 23
Monte Carlo, 22
predictability of, 21
probabilistic, 21, 22
realism of, 9–10
simple, 18–20
specification of, 3
suggested developments of, 36
SMF, 84–96, 125–161
SMG, 169
Smith, J. R., and Golden, P. A., 176
Solent Simulations, 170
Strategic people, 170
STRATGAME, 166
SUB-ARCTIC SURVIVAL, 167
THE SUPER STOCKING COMPANY, 164
Stainton Associates, 170
STRATEGY!, 175
Strat*X, 171, 172, 176
Suppliers of simulations, 162–177
System dynamics, 74

Team roles, 118–119
Teamworking skills, development of, 111
Thatcher, D., and Robinson, J., 19

Theory in use, 39, 41, 43
Thorelli, H., 177
TOPSIM, 174
Total Business Services, 171
TOWER OF BABEL, 172
TYCOON, 167

Understanding (Systems) Ltd., 171
Uses of simulations:
  in Austria, 172
  in Australia, 32–33
  case studies of, 110–124
  in developing countries, 114
  for developing teamworking skills, 111
  for exploring the business context, 110–111
  for exploring business policy, 2, 111–113
  in France, 172
  in Germany, 172
  for hospital training, 113–114
  for land use studies, 19–20
  in the Netherlands, 174
  for understanding those with physical disabilities, 19
  for research purposes, 117–121
  for social studies, 19–20
  for self-discovery, 19
  in the UK, 32–37, 114–116, 162–172
  in the USA, 32, 174–177
  for various purposes, 124
  in Yugoslavia, 177
Using a Simulation *see* Running a simulation

THE VALUE OF T, 164
Van Ensor, E., Ruderman, M., and Phillips, A. D., 117

Weber, H., 173
Wessex Training Services, 172
Wind tunnels as an example of a simulation, 8
WINWIN, 164
Witness, 77
Wolfe, J., 53
THE WORLDWIDE SIMULATION EXERCISE, 175

Further titles in the McGraw-Hill Training Series

THE BUSINESS OF TRAINING
Achieving Success in Changing World Markets
Trevor Bentley   ISBN 0-07-707328-2

EVALUATING TRAINING EFFECTIVENESS
Translating Theory into Practice
Peter Bramley   ISBN 0-07-707331-2

DEVELOPING EFFECTIVE TRAINING SKILLS
Tony Pont   ISBN 0-07-707383-5

MAKING MANAGEMENT DEVELOPMENT WORK
Achieving Success in the Nineties
Charles Margerison   ISBN 0-07-707382-7

MANAGING PERSONAL LEARNING AND CHANGE
A Trainer's Guide
Neil Clark   ISBN 0-07-707344-4

HOW TO DESIGN EFFECTIVE TEXT-BASED OPEN
LEARNING:
A Modular Course
Nigel Harrison   ISBN 0-07-707355-X

HOW TO DESIGN EFFECTIVE COMPUTER BASED
TRAINING:
A Modular Course
Nigel Harrison   ISBN 0-07-707354-1

HOW TO SUCCEED IN EMPLOYEE DEVELOPMENT
Moving from Vision to Results
Ed Moorby   ISBN 0-07-707459-9

USING VIDEO IN TRAINING AND EDUCATION
Ashly Pinnington   ISBN 0-07-707384-3

TRANSACTIONAL ANALYSIS FOR TRAINERS
Julie Hay   ISBN 0-07-707470-X